W9-BFU-436

PICASSO

and the *Weeping Women*

PICASSO and the

Weeping Women

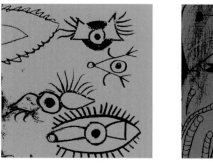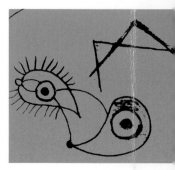

Weeping Women

The Years of Marie-Thérèse Walter & Dora Maar

ND 553 .P5 A4 1994
Freeman, Judi
Picasso and the weeping
women. WITHDRAWN

Judi Freeman

RITTER LIBRARY
BALDWIN-WALLACE COLLEGE

Los Angeles County Museum of Art

RIZZOLI
NEW YORK

Exhibition itinerary:

Los Angeles County
Museum of Art
13 February – 1 May 1994

The Metropolitan
Museum of Art,
New York
12 June – 4 September 1994

Editor:
Thomas Frick

Designer:
Amy McFarland

Photographer:
Barbara Lyter

Production assistant:
Agnes Sexty

Printer:
Nissha Printing Co., Ltd.,
Kyoto, Japan

This exhibition is made possible by **PaineWebber**.

Copublished by the Los
Angeles County Museum
of Art, 5905 Wilshire
Blvd., Los Angeles,
California 90036, and
Rizzoli International
Publications, Inc., 300
Park Avenue South, New
York, New York 10010.

Copyright © 1994
Museum Associates, Los
Angeles County Museum
of Art. All rights reserved
under international copy-
right conventions. No
part of this book may be
reproduced or utilized in
any form or by any means,
electronic or mechanical,
including photocopying,
recording, or by any information storage and
retrieval system without
permission in writing from
the publishers.

All works of Pablo Picasso:
© 1994 Succession Pablo
Picasso/Artists Rights
Society (ARS), New York

ISBN: 0-8478-1800-4
(Hardbound)
Second printing

Front cover/ jacket:
Weeping Woman, 26
October 1937 (fig. 83)

Back cover/jacket and
Half-title page:
Details: *Head of a Bull with
Studies of Eyes*, 20 May
1937 (fig. 20); *Head of a
Woman*, 20 May 1937 (fig.
21); *Weeping Woman*, 3
June 1937 (fig. 34)

Title page:
Detail: *Weeping Woman*, 3
June 1937 (fig. 34)

Foreword:
Detail: *Weeping Woman
with Handkerchief*, 26 June
1937 (fig. 47)

Sponsor's statement
page:
Detail: *Portrait of Dora
Maar*, 23 November 1937
(fig.129)

Photo sources
and credits:
Unless otherwise indi-
cated, all photographs are
reproduced courtesy of the
lenders.

Lou Meluso: figs. 1–2, 4; ©
Photo R.M.N.: figs. 9–10,
57–58, 60–63, 68, 75,
78–80, 86, 89, 93, 95, 102,
106–7, 127–28; Archivo
fotográfico Museo
Nacional Centro de Arte
Reina Sofia: figs. 11–18,
20–25, 27–38, 40–42,

66–67, 71–74; courtesy
Cahiers d'art archives: figs.
19, 22, 26; Barbara Lyter,
LACMA: figs. 47, 77; cour-
tesy Francese Catala-Roca:
fig. 48; courtesy Mission
du Patrimoine
Photographique, Paris; and
© Ministère de la Culture,
Paris: fig. 49;
Calveras/Sagristà: figs.
50–51; courtesy Library of
The Tate Gallery, London:
fig. 53; The Museum of
Modern Art, New York,
Film Stills Archive: figs.
54–56; reproduced by
courtesy of the Trustees,
The National Gallery,
London: fig. 69; permis-
sion courtesy of National
Gallery of Victoria,
Melbourne: fig. 76; cour-
tesy Richard Gray Gallery,
Chicago: fig. 85; courtesy
Billy Klüver and Julie
Martin: fig. 87; Malcolm
Varon: fig. 96; Hickey and
Robertson, Houston: fig.
99; John Webb: figs. 100,
143; Geoffrey Clements,
New York: fig. 103;
Musée Picasso, Paris: fig.
106; Lee Fatheree: fig. 108;
Michael Cavanagh and
Kevin Montague: fig. 115;
courtesy Man Ray Trust,
Paris: fig. 126; Lee Miller
Archives, Chiddingly,
England: figs. 130–32;
Paul Hester, Houston: fig.
137; courtesy The
Museum of Modern Art,

Library of Congress
Cataloging-in-Publication
Data:

Freeman, Judi
     Picasso and the weep-
ing women: the years of
Marie-Thérèse Walter and
Dora Maar/Judi
Freeman.—1st ed.
     P. CM.
     "Exhibition itinerary:
Los Angeles County
Museum of Art,
February 13–May 1, 1994;
The Metropolitan
Museum of Art, New
York, June 12–September
4, 1994; Art Institute of
Chicago, October 8,
1994–January 8, 1995"—
T.p. verso.
     Includes bibliographi-
cal references.
     ISBN 0-8478-1800-4
     ISBN 0-85787-169-0
(LACMA paperback)
     1. Picasso, Pablo,
1881-1973—Exhibitions.
2.Women in art—
Exhibitions. 3. Walter,
Marie-Thérèse, 1909-
1977. 4. Marr, Dora.
5. Artists' models—
France—Biography. I. Los
Angeles County Museum
of Art. II. Metropolitan
Museum of Art (New
York, NY). III. Art
Institute of Chicago.
IV. Title.
ND553. P5A4 1994
709´.2 —DC20
93-38179
                              CIP

Contents

I

"And this chicken is a chicken."

II

"...Picasso sends us our death notice..."

III

"...by virtue of what cold nonchalance can you detach yourself...?"

IV

"...the Muses are women."

V

"...the gift of metamorphosis."

Foreword

"The first image I ever saw of Picasso's work," David Hockney wrote, "was the *Weeping Woman*. I can never forget it."[1] He was referring to the version of 26 October 1937, now in the collection of the Tate Gallery (and reproduced on the cover of this volume as well as within), which he encountered on one of the frequent occasions it was shown in London during the 1950s and 1960s.

Southern Californians have had the opportunity for a similarly indelible experience. Since 1955 the Los Angeles County Museum of Art has had the exceptional good fortune to own Picasso's *Weeping Woman with Handkerchief* (26 June 1937), a generous gift of Mr. and Mrs. Thomas Mitchell. It is particularly appropriate that this museum has organized the exhibition *Picasso and the Weeping Women*. We are delighted that The Metropolitan Museum of Art and the Art Institute of Chicago are partners in our venture, and that this exhibition will be seen by audiences in Los Angeles, New York, and Chicago.

There has never before been an exhibition devoted to the theme of the weeping woman in Picasso's oeuvre, nor has there been one that places these images in the continuum of his depictions of women in general from the late 1920s through the early 1940s. The importance of Picasso's intense and repeated explorations of this striking motif has been cast into shadow by the monumental painting to which they are inextricably linked: *Guernica*.

Judi Freeman conceived and researched the exhibition and wrote the present volume during her tenure as associate curator of twentieth-century art at the Los Angeles County Museum of Art. During the summer of 1993 Ms. Freeman became Joan Whitney Payson Curator at the Portland Museum of Art in Maine and continued to serve as curator of the exhibition. She has brought scholarship, passion, and unflagging perseverance to this project during the past three years. For her efforts we are most thankful.

Picasso and the Weeping Women has received generous funding from PaineWebber, and we gratefully acknowledge the early commitment of Donald B. Marron, chairman and chief executive officer, and PaineWebber's board of directors. We deeply appreciate PaineWebber's

1. David Hockney, *Picasso* (Madras and New York: Hanuman Books, 1990), 9.

enlightened patronage. Many of the foreign loans were indemnified by the Federal Council on the Arts and the Humanities.

The generosity of the lenders to the exhibition, who have agreed to share their Picassos with the public for nearly a year, has been exceptional. We offer our sincere thanks to each of them. The early support of Nicholas Serota, director, the Tate Gallery; Maria de Corral, director, Museo Nacional Centro de Arte Reina Sofía; and Gerard Regnier, director, Musée Picasso was extremely important to the project.

Picasso and the Weeping Women is an important new look at an artist who never fails to richly reward our attention. We hope that our efforts will encourage additional examinations of individual themes in Picasso's work in so that a more complete picture of this twentieth-century genius may emerge.

Stephanie Barron

Coordinator of Curatorial Affairs

Los Angeles County Museum of Art

February 1994

Sponsor's statement

PaineWebber is proud to sponsor the exhibition and tour of *Picasso and the Weeping Women*, organized by the Los Angeles County Museum of Art.

Although Pablo Picasso's long and prolific career has been the subject of many exhibitions, *Picasso and the Weeping Women* is the first to focus on a brief but crucial aspect of the work of perhaps the greatest artist of the twentieth century. As a group, these remarkable portraits reveal in a way rarely seen before Picasso's fascination with and his artistic transformation of the human face.

It is this pursuit of independent thought and gift for limitless expression that we at PaineWebber salute. PaineWebber has long been dedicated to supporting the arts. We are pleased that this exhibition and book will offer fresh insights into one of the most prodigious and expressive artistic geniuses of our time.

Donald B. Marron
Chairman and Chief Executive Officer
PaineWebber Group Inc.

"And this chicken

is a chicken."

"But this bull is a bull and this horse is a horse. There's a sort of bird, too, a chicken or a pigeon. I don't remember now exactly what it is, on a table. And this chicken is a chicken. Sure, they're symbols. But it isn't up to a painter to create the symbols; otherwise, it would be better if he wrote them out in so many words instead of painting them. The public who look at the picture see in the horse and the bull symbols which they inter-pret as they understand them. There are some animals. These are animals, massacred animals. That's all, so far as I'm concerned. It's up to the public to see what it wants to see."

— Picasso in 1947, commenting on *Guernica* [1]

*T*he faces of Picasso's weeping women, portraits created principally during 1937, are among the most wrenching in the history of art. These bust-length portraits are close-up embodiments of varying degrees of grief and emotional agony. Their appearance in 1937 is symptomatic of their role as emblems of the upheavals seizing Europe during the tumultuous years preceding World War II; their completion at a time when Picasso's personal life was in considerable turmoil points to an autobiographical dimension as well.

"Sure, they're symbols," observed Picasso, responding to a question about the motifs in his 1937 painting *Guernica*. "It's up to the public to see what it wants to see," he said, thereby encouraging many interpretations. The weeping women in particular readily lend themselves to varied readings. Executed mostly during a concentrated period between January and November 1937, the nearly sixty pictures on this theme have been inextricably linked to Picasso's mammoth antiwar canvas, *Guernica*, completed in June of that year. *Guernica* was indeed central to the conception and working out of the motif. However, although Picasso produced significant numbers of weeping women images as part of his preparation for *Guernica*, there are in fact no individual weeping women in the final version of the mural. After Picasso completed *Guernica* he abandoned its motifs, but remained attached to the weeping women, which he began to paint, draw, and etch in earnest in the months that followed.

Based solely on such evidence one could easily believe that Picasso found the weeping women to be more searing and memorable emblems for the tragedy of war than was the complex composition of *Guernica*. This may indeed be true. But the coincidence of Picasso's gripping motif and the turbulent times in his personal affairs cannot be minimized. Comparisons between the weeping women's faces and those of his mistresses Marie-Thérèse Walter and Dora Maar, as well as his estranged wife, Olga Koklova, demonstrate the presence of attributes of each of these women in the construction of the image.

Page 12: detail
Head of a Woman
(Figure 96)

At the age of seventeen Marie-Thérèse Walter became Picasso's principal mistress; she remained so from 1927 through 1936, when she was essentially replaced by Dora Maar, a photographer active in surrealist circles. Although Walter gave birth to Picasso's first daughter, Maya, in 1935, she was unhappily but irrevocably replaced by Maar in Picasso's affections by the end of the next year. Picasso remained married throughout these years to Koklova, a former dancer with the Ballets Russes, though he had been separated from her since the early 1930s.

Maar's dark features, her prominent forehead, and her elongated hands with sharpened fingernails appear in many of the weeping women, while Walter's rounded face and almond-shaped eyes pervade others. The jagged teeth and pointed tongues characteristic of a number of these portraits have a lengthier pedigree: these features dominate tortured images of Koklova that Picasso created from 1927 through 1929, during the early years of his relationship with Walter.

Picasso scholarship is characterized by innumerable discussions of symbolism. Virtually every one of Picasso's pictures contains a character (or cast of characters) alluding to something beyond its frame. Bulls and minotaurs are said to represent Picasso himself; horses, though male, symbolize woman.[2] The sitter with the elongated face, often present in Picasso's paintings from the blue period, is said to be the ghostly apparition of the childhood friend who committed suicide, Carlos Casagemas.[3] The words *ma jolie*, appearing in several of Picasso's cubist paintings and drawings, refer to his lover Eva (Marcelle Humbert).[4] The bits of newsprint that paper the cubist collages are in fact deliberately excerpted texts that allude to important and vexing issues of the day.[5] All of these assertions have prompted considerable debate, in large part because Picasso personally never sanctioned one view over another. Many writers have attributed the fertile field of debate that his art inspires simply to Picasso's genius. Satisfied with that "explanation," they refuse to speculate further, thereby increasing the aura around his oeuvre and its meaning.

At the time of this writing little more than twenty years have passed since Picasso's death in 1973. Picasso scholarship is still essentially in its infancy. The pre–World War I work has been relatively well served. His blue, rose, and harlequin periods have received careful recent analysis, and his cubist years have been the focus of considerable and significant research. There is, however, a marked difference in both the quantity and sophistication of writing on the post–World War I portion of his career; though there have been admirable studies devoted to Picasso's classical and surrealist phases of the 1920s and 1930s, and to his writings, which began in 1935, further investigation of these periods in his career is sorely needed. There never has been a study devoted solely to the weeping women, for example, chiefly because discussion of these works has been subsumed by analysis of *Guernica*.

In general the most prominent writers on Picasso have been men acquainted with him during the latter half of his career; these include John Richardson, Alfred H. Barr, Jr., William S. Rubin, William S. Lieberman, Douglas Cooper, Pierre Daix, Dominique Bozo, and Werner Spies. Many met him while he was living with Françoise Gilot (from 1946 through 1953); all knew him during his second marriage, to Jacqueline Roque (from 1954 until his death in 1973). Almost unanimously they confess an awe and admiration for the man, his stamina, and his magnetism. Inevitably they refer to his life when discussing his art. The two volumes on Picasso by the Museum of Modern Art's Barr are rare attempts at dealing with the artist's work formally and analytically without dwelling on his biography.[6] Nonetheless Barr confessed to professor Henry Hope while completing his second book that there were other subjects related to Picasso's work equally in need of examination:

I think it is probably true that Picasso's relation to women and to womanhood is of fundamental importance to his art, but I do not feel competent or even free to speculate at the present time without making foolish and impertinent errors and, incidentally, without incurring Picasso's enmity, which I wish to avoid both for personal and institutional reasons.[7]

Barr too was under the spell of a figure of enormous stature; his personal contact with the man, like that of his fellow Picasso scholars and biographers, necessarily colored what he would or would not say about the work. Inevitably conversations with such scholars prompt remarks prefaced by the phrase "as Pablo told me," and so any discussion definitively ends. This is not intended as a rejection of the work of these scholars—indeed far from it—but rather as an essential note of caution about their objectivity.

Picasso's work is so interlaced with his personal biography that phases in his career are often labeled by scholars according to the places where he worked (Boisgeloup, Dinard, Royan, Mougins, Cannes, Juan-les-Pins) or the women with whom he was involved.[8] His neoclassicism of the twenties is from "the Olga years"; the bathers of the late twenties and early thirties represent "the Marie-Thérèse era"; the portraits of the late forties date from "the Françoise period."

Is discussion of personal biography mandatory in examinations of other, equally renowned twentieth-century figures? A book on John F. Kennedy's career could be convincing without mentions of his wife and children. A credible study of Leonard Bernstein would not require exploring his religion or his marital history. Can anyone instantly recall anything about Albert Einstein's personal life? Yet treatment of Picasso's career without reference to one or another of his mistresses, wives, and models is inconceivable. If such a work did exist, it would be critiqued for such an omission.[9] An overwhelming number of Picasso's images are depictions of women; these did not appear from nowhere. They require identification, and the significance of their relation to him needs to be explored. Two of the seven principal women involved with Picasso wrote memoirs while he was still alive; a third has recently "spoken" through a selective biography of her.[10] Upon Picasso's death the lack of a will resulted in internecine struggles among members of his family, again exposing details of his personal life to the public eye.

"Biography," as Janet Malcolm has astutely observed in her essay on the writer Sylvia Plath,

is the medium through which the remaining secrets of the famous dead are taken from them and dumped out in full view of the world. The biographer at work, indeed, is like the professional burglar, breaking into a house, rifling through certain drawers that he has good reason to think contain the jewelry and the money, and triumphantly bearing his loot away.

There is a kind of unspoken "collusion" between the reader and the biographer "in an excitingly forbidden undertaking: tiptoeing down the corridor together, to stand in front of the bedroom door and try to peep through the keyhole."[11]

Picasso's choice of images makes such study inevitable. The issue worth probing is not whether the weeping women are specific metamorphoses of Koklova, Walter, and Maar, but, more pertinently, what was it about Picasso, these women, and the times in general that made it necessary for him to create such imagery? How did he develop the individual motifs constituting these wrenching, torturous expressions? Why did he mask so many of their references and sources? How can we relate these faces to Picasso's feelings about his personal situation and his attitudes toward the rapidly changing political landscape in 1937?

Picasso's figures are often expressionless; their gestures and poses suggest what they are doing and, sometimes, how they feel about it. Openly expressive, the weeping women are an exception. Indeed they are perhaps the most emotive of any of Picasso's human figures. (Only his animals and his minotaurs appear in greater distress.) Intricately crafted facial and bodily features individually contribute to the total effect of these potent images.

Picasso was the consummate metaphorical artist, using one thing to mean many others. He buried his personal passions in a visual code. Whether a bulging bowl of fruit, a skull, or a bird in flight, every one of his images refers to something else. His language was the twentieth-century version of that of Hieronymus Bosch or Pieter Bruegel the Elder, with their emblem book–derived references requiring meticulous detection and interpretation for full comprehension. To understand Picasso the viewer must build a lexicon of the artist's motifs and then translate it into something personally comprehensible.

I debated several approaches to this study of the weeping women. The faces haunted me but they seemed uninhabited. This convinced me that if the weeping woman's face can indeed be identified, then it is a composite and not drawn from any individual. If I could identify a single personality (as Eunice Lipton so brilliantly "found" Victorine Meurent in her groundbreaking volume *Alias Olympia*),[12] I would have conceived a being heretofore unknown in Picasso studies. Instead I have deciphered the weeping women by extracting single features, examining them, and then reassessing them as parts of a whole. This is the approach of Lydia Gasman in her pioneering, incisive study of Picasso's work of the 1920s and 1930s, to which the present volume is enormously indebted. She advocates the analysis of what she terms Picasso's "ideograms," signature images of "teeth, jaws, eyes, the tongue, feet, hands, fingernails, bones, etc." which "often convey the central meaning of the works in which they appear."[13] The weeping women compose an identifiable body of work, created over a relatively short period of time, that lends itself to such a model of analysis.

In this study I attempt to avoid many of the myths of Picasso that have governed so much of the writing about him. Yes, Picasso was prolific, gifted, a chameleon who, if such things can be charted, must have done little other than eaten, had sex, and made several works of art on any given day. Yes, Picasso devoured the people, the events, and the things around him with great passion and transformed these into his art. But the fact that this passion ruled his art and life does not mean that his work cannot be analytically interpreted, nor does it mean that by doing so the power and the magic of that work is lost or eclipsed. If we can identify a code that enables us to read his work (even if that code must be newly interpreted by each viewer), then we can establish linkages between different phases in Picasso's career and between widely divergent images. In short, such a method allows us to come to an understanding of Picasso, even if that understanding will for the foreseeable future be subject to endless refinement and revision.

Notes

1. Picasso, quoted by Daniel-Henry Kahnweiler in a letter to Alfred H. Barr, Jr., received on 29 May 1947 and read by Barr at the *Guernica* symposium at The Museum of Modern Art on 25 November 1947. Typescript of symposium on *Guernica*, The Museum of Modern Art, 25 November 1947, 13. (Museum of Modern Art Library, New York)

2. Typical of the many assertions of this view is Roland Penrose's articulate discussion "Beauty and the Monster" in Penrose and Golding 1973, 101–25. For full citations see bibliography.

3. For the most reasoned discussion of Casagemas's appearance in Picasso's work see Theodore Reff, "Themes of Love and Death in Picasso's Early Work," in Penrose and Golding 1973, 5–30; especially 9–17.

4. See for example Paris 1955, no. 30; Rubin 1972, 69–70; Rubin and Armstrong 1992, 109.

5. See the seminal 1971 article by Robert Rosenblum, "Picasso and the Typography of Cubism," in Penrose and Golding 1973, 33–47; as well as Leighten 1989; and Poggi 1992.

6. Barr 1939, 1946.

7. Letter from Alfred H. Barr, Jr., to Henry Hope, 21 November 1946. The Museum of Modern Art archives: Alfred H. Barr, Jr., Papers; Picasso II. Henry Hope in 1946 was professor of fine arts at Indiana University, Bloomington, Indiana. He would organize The Museum of Modern Art's 1949 Georges Braque and 1954 Jacques Lipschitz exhibitions for Barr. I thank Rona Roob, archivist at The Museum of Modern Art, New York, for her help with the Barr papers.

8. Such approaches govern the installation of the permanent collection of the Musée Picasso in Paris.

9. The scholarship on Henri Matisse, for example, suffers from just such neglect. Many scholars correctly observe that Matisse's preferred subject was that of a female model in his studio. Who these models were and Matisse's attitudes toward them are subjects that have remained shrouded. One could argue that this is partially the result of his family's efforts (first his daughter, Marguérite Duthuit, then his grandchildren), whose restrictions on access to information about Matisse's personal life have limited any serious scholarly discussion of it. I can well recall a conversation I had while working in the Matisse archives during the preparation of my 1990 exhibition *The Fauve Landscape*. Publication of Arianna Stassinopoulos Huffington's superficial book of tabloid journalism, *Picasso: Creator and*

Destroyer, had just occurred, prompting considerable speculation and titillation over details of Picasso's personal life. Claude Duthuit, Matisse's grandson, and his wife, Barbara, understandably bemoaned the situation of the artist as subject for bawdy biography and reiterated their own insistence on limiting access to Matisse's personal papers. What had happened to Picasso, they said, would not happen to Matisse. The dichotomy between the right to privacy and the need for public and scholarly access to factual knowledge, an everpresent question regarding the lives of people in the public eye, is clearly germane.

10. See Olivier 1988; Gilot and Lake 1964; and Lord 1993.

11. Janet Malcolm, "The Silent Woman," *The New Yorker,* 23 and 30 August 1993, 86. I am grateful to Maria Porges for referring me to this essay.

12. Eunice Lipton, *Alias Olympia: A Woman's Search for Manet's Notorious Model and Her Own Desire.* New York: Charles Scribner's Sons, 1992.

13. See Gasman 1981, 661.

"...*Picasso sends us*

"To take up a pen, line up words as if they could

add anything to Picasso's Guernica, is the most

useless of undertakings. In the black-and-white

rectangle of ancient tragedy, Picasso sends us our

death notice: everything we love is going to die,

and that is why right now it is important to die,

our death notice..."

and that is why right now it is important that

everything we love be summed up into something

unforgettably beautiful, like the shedding of so

many tears of farewell."

—Michel Leiris, 1937 [1]

On 8 January 1937 Picasso began etching his *Dream and Lie of Franco*.[2]
Each of the two prints was divided, comic-strip-style, into three rows of
three scenes. Picasso worked on them from left to right, but as printed
they read from right to left. He completed all but four of the eighteen
scenes by the end of the next day. In the first scene (fig. 1, upper right)
Franco appears as a composite scarecrow/jellyfish with enormous tentacles and an elephantine head. He is astride a disemboweled horse. Next
he has dismounted and exposes his hairy scrotum and an enormous penis.
In the third frame he raises a pickax to a female bust. In the fourth, he
stands in the foreground, clad in a traditional Spanish mantilla and comb
and holding a fan, with a city on the distant horizon. A bull, symbolizing Spain generally and the Spanish Popular Front's resistance specifically,

Figure 1

Dream and Lie of Franco
(scenes 1–9)
8 January 1937
(with aquatint added
25 May 1937)
Etching and aquatint
on paper
12 3/8 x 16 5/8 in.
(31.4 x 42.1 cm)
Collection of the
Grunwald Center for
the Graphic Arts,
University of California,
Los Angeles.
Gift of Mr. and Mrs.
Fred Grunwald

Page 22: detail
Head of a Horse
(Figure 12)

CHAPTER II

Figure 2

Dream and Lie of Franco

(scenes 10–18)

8 January 1937

(with aquatint added 25 May 1937 and final four panels added 7 June 1937)

Etching and aquatint on paper

12 ³⁄₈ x 16 ⁵⁄₈ in.

(31.4 x 42.1 cm)

Collection of the Grunwald Center for the Graphic Arts, University of California, Los Angeles.

Gift of Mr. and Mrs. Fred Grunwald

attacks him in the fifth scene. Kneeling at a makeshift altar surrounded by barbed wire, Franco prays in the sixth frame. In the seventh he gives birth to an array of snakes and disembodied heads. He strangles and lances his horse in the next scene, so that by the ninth he no longer rides astride an animal but has been metamorphosed into half-monster, half-pig. In the tenth scene, beginning the second plate (fig. 2), Franco devours his dead horse's innards. The remnants of battle appear in the next two frames: a wounded woman lies on the ground amid burning buildings in scene eleven, while a dead warrior and horse dominate scene twelve.

Scene thirteen is a bust-length portrait. Franco, no longer the clean-shaven monster of panels one through ten, now is scruffy and

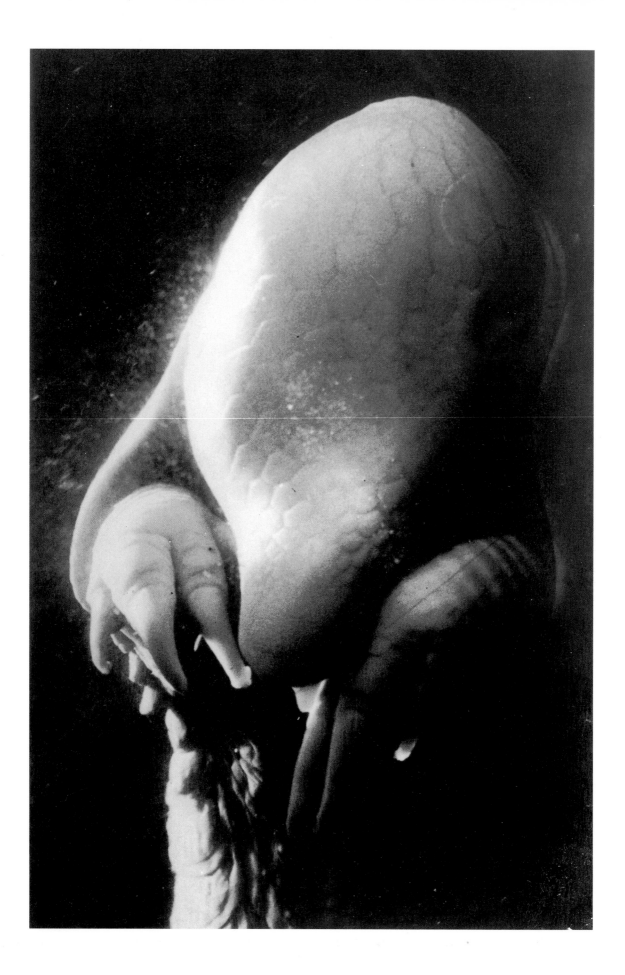

Figure 3
Dora Maar
Portrait of Ubu
1936
Gelatin silver photograph
7 ¹⁄₈ x 4 ¹⁄₂ in.
(18.1 x 11.4 cm)
National Gallery of
Australia, Canberra.
Purchased 1987

hairy, an even more grotesque specter. He resembles a flayed animal or a caricature of Ubu Roi, the protagonist of Alfred Jarry's eponymous play, and is not dissimilar to Dora Maar's 1936 close-up photograph that she titled *Portrait of Ubu* (fig. 3). Both Picasso and Maar were fascinated by the story of Ubu Roi, and he makes several appearances in Picasso's oeuvre (see fig. 70, for example). Here Franco comes face-to-face with the head of a bull. In the next frame Franco's head (now mostly shaven) is appended to the body of a disemboweled horse; he is confronted by the angry bull. This scene contains the densest and most violent activity on the second plate. Picasso completed the final four frames five months later, on 7 June. Dramatically different from the previous fourteen, these last scenes contain victims of Franco's wartime atrocities. Frame fifteen (fig. 4) depicts a weeping woman, hands reaching upward and hair disheveled, with burning phallic forms in the distance. A wailing mother holds her dead child as she flees from a burning house in frame sixteen. Frame seven-

Figure 4
Detail: scene 15 of
Dream and Lie of Franco

teen is a closeup of a fallen couple—the dead warrior from scene twelve and the female bust from scene three—caught in an embrace. Scene eighteen is an elaborated version of sixteen. Here two terrified children cling to their distraught mother as she stands before her fallen husband.

The prose poem by Picasso accompanying the two prints in the published folio vividly evokes images that underscore the horrors of the attacks of Franco and his forces: "swords of ill-omened octopuses dishrag of hairs from tonsures standing in the middle of the frying pan,"[3] writes Picasso at the beginning of his text. His images become increasingly grotesque: "beauty products from the garbage truck—rape of the ladies-in-waiting in tears and in large tears—on shoulders the coffin stuffed with sausages and mouths...lantern of lice where the dog lies knot of rats hiding place of the palace of old rags—the flags that fry in the frying pan writhe in the black of the sauce of the ink spilled in the drops of blood that shoot him."[4] Sounds reach a crescendo:

cries of children cries of women cries of birds cries of flowers cries of wood and of stones cries of bricks cries of furniture of beds of chairs of curtains of pans of cats and of papers cries of odors that scratch themselves cries of smoke pecking at the neck of the cries that boil in the cauldron and of the rain of birds that floods the sea.[5]

Figure 5

Study of Women's Heads
22 January 1937
Pencil on blue paper
10 ⁵⁄₈ x 8 ¹⁄₄ in.
(27 x 21 cm)
Picasso estate

Clearly Picasso's preoccupation with *gritos*—cries, screams, howls, shrieks—increased between January and June. He obsessively wrote in his notebook nearly every day beginning 25 January and continuing through the month of February. The texts are laced with powerful sensory allusions: the odors of flowers or perfume, the textures of liquids, the colors of things, the inflections of music. A verbal permutation introduces his entry of 20 February: "raging toothache in the eyes of the sun pique—pique raging sun-ache of the teeth in the eyes—eyes in the teeth pique of raging sun-ache pique eyes in the teeth of toothache—of the sun pique of raging eyes flower."[6]

Just as this entry explores different combinations of the same elements, so too does his study of female heads (fig. 5). He captures these misshapen faces in various configurations. Within each head floats a pair of eyes, almond-shaped slivers punctured by circles filled with dots. Many of the heads have snouts in place of noses, chunky, bulging projections of flesh. All have nostrils reduced to short strokes. Most have mouths; some of these mouths consist of elongated ovals, while others are gaping orifices. Some are filled with teeth, usually square but occasionally rounded. From between several sets of teeth, knifelike tongues protrude.

Figure 6
Rape
22 January 1937
Pencil on paper
8 ½ x 10 ⅞ in.
(21.5 x 27.5 cm)
Picasso estate

These women are clearly related to the weeping women. None has tears, but all have other features that will be quoted in the weeping women images. All allude to women contorted by violence and horrific pain. On the very same day, 22 January, Picasso drew an extremely graphic rape scene on a similar scale (fig. 6). The intensity of emotion contained in the weeping women could easily be excerpted from a violent scene of this nature. The rapist has a gnarled, monstrous, animallike head, identical to the one on the upper right of the sheet of women's heads. The victim's face is that of an animal in agony. Her mouth is a large oval, a dark hole from which presumably a piercing scream of astonishing intensity emanates, with circumferential teeth pointing toward the center.

Tears and cries of pain, as features of the face, were not exploited by Picasso alone. His preoccupations were shared by his contemporaries as well as by previous generations of Spanish artists. A tradition of weeping women exists in Spanish religious sculpture, particularly in statues of the Virgin Mary. The *mater dolorosa* was a favored theme with sixteenth- and seventeenth-century Spanish painters.

Figure 7
Joan Miró
Persons Haunted by a Bird
1938
Gouache, crayon,
watercolor and charcoal
on paper
16 ⅛ x 13 in.
(41 x 33 cm)
The Art Institute
of Chicago,
Gift of the
Peter B. Bensinger
Charitable Trust

Among contemporary artists there is an unmistakable stylistic echo of Picasso's verses for *Dream and Lie of Franco* (and his subsequent notebook jottings) in the 1937 poetry of Joan Miró:

The flaming tree of the peacock's tail that bites the snouts of bats smiling before the charred corpse of my grandmother who was buried by a dance of transparent glass nightingales with rocket wings who dance the sardana *around the phosphorescent carcass while pecking with the gold of their pincers the metal seeds of silver cypresses rushing down in waterfalls from the grandmother's big toe.*[7]

Miró wrote this on 2 October 1937, using phrases reminiscent in both style and substance of Picasso's "raging toothache in the eyes of the sun pique." Miró drew a sheet of heads (fig. 7) that sit atop bodies compara-

Figure 8
Julio González
Head ("The Snail")
c. 1935
Wrought iron
17 ¾ x 7 ¹¹⁄₁₆ x 15 ¼ in.
(45.1 x 19.5 x 38.7 cm)
The Museum of Modern
Art, New York.
Purchase

ble to those in Picasso's *Rape*; they open their mouths to scream, they crane their necks to see, they gape in amazement. Such abbreviated, organically inspired forms appear also in the work of fellow Spaniard Julio González; his *Head* of 1935 (fig. 8) is an iron arc interrupted by short strands of hair at the very top, a gaping mouth with shardlike teeth at the bottom, and a looming eye with long lashes at the center. This reductive sculpture contains a pathos akin to any of Picasso's studies on the sheet of women's heads.

Figure 9

Bather by a Cabana
Skipping Rope
6 February 1937
Pencil on paper
6 ⅞ x 10 ¼ in.
(17.5 x 26 cm)
Musée Picasso, Paris
(MP 1173)

The *Rape* and *Study of Women's Heads* mark an unusually intense involvement with violent imagery during January 1937. Picasso's predilection for the subjects of these drawings was a fitting preparation for the invitation that he received in January, from representatives of the Spanish republican government, to design a large mural for the Spanish pavilion at the International Exposition in Paris that summer.[8] His sympathies for the Spanish republican cause were clear in the equally violent *Dream and Lie of Franco*. Early in February he returned to the

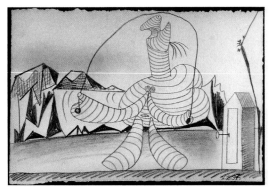

scarecrowlike figures from *Dream*. Now devoid of Franco's menacing features, these were transformed into bathers (fig. 9). In his effort to find an allegorical theme to explore for the Spanish pavilion, Picasso incorporated characteristics of these bathers into a series of works he embarked on in April depicting the artist and his model in the studio.[9] On 18 and 19 April he drew at least fourteen sketches, trying to work out the compositional elements. The most revelatory was the sixth in the group (fig. 10), in which two reclining nudes are contorted and elongated, their heads wrapped within their arms. This drawing—with its highly detailed and exaggerated studies of individual body parts—holds the greatest suggestion of tension and violence of any in the series. Along the left side of the sheet Picasso lavished great detail on certain key body parts: an eyeball; a pointed tongue protruding between jagged teeth and a pair of lips; twisted fingers seen from the side, front, and back; a nose with pronounced nostrils; an erect nipple and its aureole.

By 1 May Picasso had abandoned his initial theme—artist and model—in favor of an allegorical encounter between bull and horse. Later he coyly observed, "My work is not symbolic...only the Guernica mural is symbolic. But in the case of the mural, that is allegoric. That's the reason I've used the horse, the bull, and so on. The mural is for the definite expression and solution of a problem and that is why I used symbolism."[10] His six initial sketches, all created that Saturday, 1 May, are experiments in different arrangements of the two animals. The third

Figure 10

The Studio VI

18 April 1937

Pencil on paper

7 ¹/₈ x 11 in.

(18 x 28 cm)

Musée Picasso, Paris

(MP 1183)

sketch (fig. 11) features several humans as well, including a woman holding a lamp and a standing, distraught form at the center right of the sheet. This figure, head tilted back and toothy mouth slightly open, is the first indication that Picasso was interested in depicting states of intense emotion in his mural.[11]

Three sketches of horses made the next day confirm his intention. One of them (fig. 12) shows an animal in agony, its tongue a sharp wedge thrust upward. The head is tilted back, the mouth is thrown open, and the massive teeth sit like stubs on the gums. In another of the sketches the teeth are neatly aligned; in this one and the third they seem about to fall out as they sit precariously on the edge of the muzzle.

One week later, on 8 May, Picasso's thoughts about the composition took a dramatic turn. New to his concept for the mural was a mother carrying the body of her wounded or dead child (fig. 13). This

RITTER LIBRARY
BALDWIN-WALLACE COLLEGE

Figure 11
*Guernica: Study
for Composition*
1 May 1937 (III)
Pencil on paper
10 ⁵⁄₈ x 8 ¹⁄₄ in.
(27 x 21 cm)
Museo Nacional Centro
de Arte Reina Sofía,
Madrid

Figure 12
Head of a Horse
2 May 1937 (I)
Oil on canvas
25 ⁵⁄₈ x 36 ¹⁄₄ in.
(65 x 92 cm)
Museo Nacional Centro
de Arte Reina Sofía,
Madrid

Figure 13

Guernica: Study for Composition
8 May 1937 (1)
Pencil on paper
9 ½ x 17 ⅞ in.
(24 x 45.5 cm)
Museo Nacional Centro
de Arte Reina Sofía,
Madrid

figure was almost certainly inspired by the news coverage of the violent events in Guernica (in the northern, Basque region of Spain) that had appeared in Paris newspapers during the previous week.[12] On Monday, 26 April, German planes from the Condor Legion acting in support of Franco's forces bombed central Guernica repeatedly. Toward the close of market day the town was overrun by fire and for the most part leveled.

Paris learned the news the following day; *L'Humanité*'s headline read: "Mille bombes incendiaires lancées par les avions de Hitler et de Mussolini réduisent en cendres la ville de Guernica" (A thousand fire-bombs dropped by Hitler's and Mussolini's planes reduce the town of Guernica to ashes). While other newspapers initially covered and then abandoned the story, *L'Humanité* vigorously pursued it. On 29 April it published a vivid account of the carnage (translated from the preceding day's London *Times*) by a British correspondent in Bilbao who had been to Guernica the day after the bombing:

At 2 a.m. to-day when I visited the town the whole of it was a horrible sight,
flaming from end to end. The reflection of the flames could be seen in the clouds
of smoke above the mountains from ten miles away. Throughout the night houses
were falling until the streets became long heaps of red impenetrable debris. Many
of the civilian survivors took the long trek from Guernica to Bilbao in antique
solid-wheeled Basque farmcarts drawn by oxen. Carts piled high with such
household possessions as could be saved from the conflagration clogged the roads
all night. Other survivors were evacuated in Government lorries, but many were
forced to remain round the burning town lying on mattresses or looking for lost
relatives and children, while units of the fire brigades and the Basque motorized
police...continued rescue work till dawn.[13]

The president of the Basque region, José Antonio Aguirre, issued a
statement reprinted in many papers:

Before God and before history that will judge us I swear that for three-and-one-
half hours German planes bombed with inconceivable destruction the undefended
civil population of Guernica, reducing the celebrated city to cinders. They pursued
with machine-gun fire the women and children who were frantically fleeing.[14]

The accounts of these horrific events ignited the passions of Popular
Front activists in France. The traditional May Day celebration in Paris
brought out more than a million demonstrators, who marched from
the Place de la République to the Bastille to express their outrage and
appeal for aid to the victims.

May Day was Picasso's first day of concerted work on the
Guernica mural. He initially expressed his reaction to the events in
Spain by using his preferred symbolic combatants: the bull and the
horse. By 8 May accounts of the individual human tragedies in Guernica
had clearly permeated his thinking. The inclusion of the mother and
child (and their consistent appearance henceforth in his scheme for the
picture) demonstrates this. In figure 13 the mother has an extended
trunk for a neck that protrudes from one long mass of flesh encircling
the body of a limp child. Her cast-back head, shown in profile, is com-

Figure 14

*Horse and Mother with
Dead Child*
8 May 1937 (II)
Pencil on paper
9 ½ x 17 ⅞ in.
(24 x 45.5 cm)
Museo Nacional Centro
de Arte Reina Sofía,
Madrid

posed of an open, toothless mouth, a slight protrusion for a nose, and two dotted ovals for eyes. Picasso drew her head in a single rapid stroke, then added lines to alter the neck slightly. This quick, self-assured gesture indicates his certainty about the face, the pose, and the emotional tone.

The motif is further elaborated in a second drawing done that day (fig. 14); a shawl, draped around the mother's head and shoulders, serves to cover the child. The child's blood stains the mother's breast and hand. She looks upward. Her face conveys the intensity of the horror. Her teeth, lips, and tongue are defined in exquisite detail; her nose is now further developed, thanks to comma-shaped nostrils; her eyes now have eyebrows. Her mouth is slightly open; she is speaking, screaming, wailing.

The next day's drawing, an ink close-up of the mother and child, provides further information (fig. 15). As Picasso lavishes greater attention on the mother, the child becomes increasingly doll-like, with abbreviated, caricatured features. The mother's mouth is open wider; her eyelids appear for the first time and define her expression; her brows are bushier and pinched together. She appears shocked but not helpless, angered but not enraged, whereas her predecessor seems dazed and

Figure 15

Mother with Dead Child

9 May 1937 (I)

Ink on paper

9 ½ x 17 ⅞ in.

(24 x 45.5 cm)

Museo Nacional Centro

de Arte Reina Sofía,

Madrid

distraught. Picasso was of course aware of the ways in which his most minor graphic decisions would alter the viewer's perception of his subject's emotions. Placed on a ladder (fig. 16), the mother looks like a recumbent dinosaur turned upright. Her head is thrown back 180 degrees. Several strokes of ink define the tears falling from her eyes. Her tongue, now rounded, dangles in her open mouth, while her teeth are studs on her lips. Her hair forms a clipped cap of strands that, like the tongue, creates an angular protrusion. All of these elements contribute, along with the extremely contorted poses of the two figures, to a sense of their physical and mental agony.

Later that day, 9 May, Picasso drew a study (fig. 17) for the mural's overall composition into which he integrated the mother with dead child. She kneels at the lower right, the child in her arms; her head is tilted backward. Her profile is minimally detailed, much like the mother in figure 13. Two other women appear in this scene. The first is an embellished version of the woman holding the lamp in figure 11.

Figure 16

Mother with Dead Child

on Ladder

9 May 1937 (III)

Pencil on paper

17 ⅞ x 9 ½ in.

(45.5 x 24 cm)

Museo Nacional Centro

de Arte Reina Sofía,

Madrid

Figure 17

*Guernica: Study for
Composition*
9 May 1937 (II)
Pencil on paper
17 ⁷/₈ x 9 ⁵/₈ in.
(45.5 x 24.5 cm)
Museo Nacional Centro
de Arte Reina Sofia,
Madrid

Now she holds a candle and stares with amazement. Her lips are parted, but she appears speechless. Her wide-open eyes and arched brows communicate her horror. The second appears at the far left, framed by a doorway. Her jagged profile and elongated neck-body resemble those of the mother with dead child at the right. The concept for all three women originated in Picasso's earlier sketches for the mother with dead child, which in turn had their origins in his many drawings of women's heads. There is a clear lineage, then, back to January 1937 (and even earlier) for these ideogrammatic women-signs.

Most of the following day, 10 May, was devoted to studies of the bull and horse, with the exception of one sketch, *Mother with Dead Child on Ladder* (v) (fig. **18**). This drawing is the first colored version of the theme, and its hues are vibrant. The mother is wide-eyed and aghast. Her mouth is a dark, gaping orifice. Her nose is less rounded and more angular than in figure 16, and her mass of hair is framed by thickly

Figure 18

*Mother with Dead
Child on Ladder*
10 May 1937 (v)
Pencil and crayon
on paper
17 ⁷/₈ x 9 ⁵/₈ in.
(45.5 x 24.5 cm)
Museo Nacional Centro
de Arte Reina Sofia,
Madrid

applied green crayon. Surrounded by saturated, intense color, she embodies a heightened, macabre violence.

On 11 May Picasso began drawing the mural itself. He translated the minute sketches of the previous weeks onto a canvas of enormous scale—more than 11 feet high by 25 feet wide. He must have changed some elements in the process of applying them to the canvas because the differences between his most recent compositional study (fig. 17) and the first version of the actual work (fig. 19) (photographed by Maar in his Grands Augustins studio) were dramatic. The stage set defined by Picasso in his 9 May study—with a flaming building on the right and a doorway on the left—is now somewhat reduced in size.[15] The doorway at the far left has disappeared. The bust-length wailing woman previously situated there has been replaced by a mother with dead child, resembling the pair that appeared in the first 8 May study. Another wailing woman, this one without a child, appears with raised arms at the far right of the canvas. The many lines running through her suggest that Picasso debated about how he would configure her. Three other women appear. One lies dead along the bottom right edge of the canvas. Another appears to kneel at center right, holding the dead woman. Her face resembles the mother in figure 17, but she looks plaintive rather than distraught or agitated. Above her is the woman holding the candle, who plays such an essential role in the final mural. The latter two are witnesses rather than emotional participants in the scene.

Over the next six days, a period of intense work, Picasso filled in sections of the canvas.[16] He began to define its dark and light areas. He added a large round sun above the wounded horse and filled the fist (which first appeared in a 19 April drawing on the theme of the artist and his model) with a sheaf of wheat. This fist would disappear when he revised the mural several days later. He slightly refined the horse's position and shifted the placement of its teeth. These were minimal changes, but within the next several days Picasso completely redrew the horse's head, inverting it.[17] Save the addition of hands to the woman at the lower right, who now appears to be running or fleeing, Picasso left the women essentially unchanged.

Figure 19
Dora Maar
Guernica, state 1
Photographed on
11 May 1937

On 20 May he turned his attention to the animals in the scene, completing four studies of the heads of the horse and the bull. In one (fig. 20) he drew numerous eyes: eyes like butterflies, insects, birds, goblets, flames. At this moment it is clear that he was considering which of these to use as the eyes of the bull, but later that day he incorporated two of them into his sketch of a woman (fig. 21). This is very probably a study for the figure at the far left of the mural as it was then conceived:

Figure 20
Head of a Bull with Studies of Eyes
20 May 1937
Pencil and gouache on paper
11 ⅜ x 9 in.
(29 x 23 cm)
Museo Nacional Centro de Arte Reina Sofía, Madrid

the mother holding the dead child. Her eyes are connected teardrop shapes; one contains a butterflylike form. Her brows are two intersecting wedges, considerably more minimal than those used in previous figures.

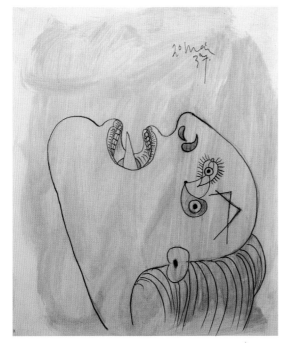

The lack of physiognomical detail in this area makes it difficult to read her expression and attitude.

Picasso provides considerably more articulation in the mouth area. Her lips are shaped and modeled; her teeth are drawn in three dimensions; her tongue is a spike. The form Picasso gives to the mouth is highly erotic. Its lips are labia, its tongue a sharpened clitoris. None of Picasso's *Guernica*-related women up to this point had mouths on which so much attention had been lavished. Her nostrils are bulbous, shaded commas, and her single ear is an enlarged version of the simplified eyes found in his January studies. Her hair is now a series of thin, dangling lines.

Figure 21

Head of a Woman
20 May 1937
Pencil and gouache
on paper
11 ³/₈ x 9 in.
(29 x 23 cm)
Museo Nacional Centro
de Arte Reina Sofía,
Madrid

Whatever Picasso was attempting in this drawing, he did not immediately incorporate it into his mural, as demonstrated by the photograph Maar took no later than 24 May (fig. 22). Much of Picasso's energy thus far had been devoted to the arrangement of the bull and the horse. The bull, with its human eyes based on the 20 May study, is turned around and now faces the woman with dead child. Picasso's completion of the dark and light areas of the canvas emphasizes the blade of the horse's tongue and the teeth standing, as they seem to, on their roots. The horse's mouth is much more menacing than the woman's in figure 21; there is clearly a different threshold for anger and violence among animals than humans. Picasso focused considerably more attention on the female figures during this phase of *Guernica*'s evolution. The hands of the figure at the far right have been completely repositioned; one remains up, the other is now down. The neck has become highly contorted. The bulbous commas of her eyes are filled

with enlarged pupils. Picasso also clothed the fleeing woman at the lower right by applying collage elements to mimic a kerchief and a floral dress. In subsequent revisions of the mural these additions were removed.

Two heads of 24 May (figs. 23–24) suggest that Picasso was continuing to explore alternatives, although these visages never appeared in the final mural. These are the first weeping heads among the preparatory drawings and paintings created for *Guernica*. Their tears are like splayed multipronged rakes. In the first (fig. 23), tears drop from each eye. Her eye sockets resemble cells with cilia; one contains a bow tie, the other a wrapped bonbon. She has dark eyebrows and a furrowed forehead. Picasso drew the contour of her face in two rapid strokes. The texture of the mouth receives considerable description; the tongue is scaled and the

Figure 22
Dora Maar
Guernica, state IV
Photographed between
20 and 24 May 1937

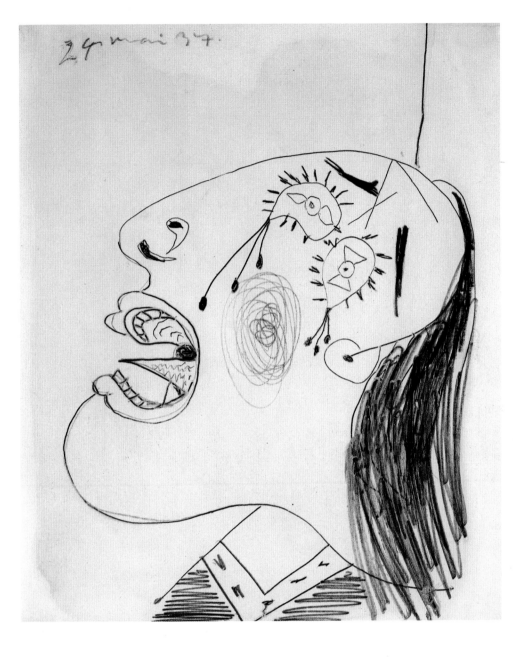

Figure 23

Weeping Woman

24 May 1937

Pencil and gouache on

paper

11 ³/₈ x 9 in.

(29 x 23 cm)

Museo Nacional Centro

de Arte Reina Sofía,

Madrid

palate is ridged. The teeth are neatly aligned and rounded. She wears makeup, or so the circular lines on her cheek suggest.

Within a single day Picasso's approach toward representing the weeping women took a new direction. In the second version of 24 May (fig. 24) the irregularly shaped face is more a mask than an observed head. It is surrounded by a mass of dark, unruly hair. Set beneath thick eyebrows, her teardrop-shaped eyes fall to either side of her face and appear to contain elaborately wrapped candies. Her tears trace random

Figure 24
Weeping Woman
24 May 1937
Pencil and gouache
on paper
11 ³/₈ x 9 in.
(29 x 23 cm)
Museo Nacional Centro
de Arte Reina Sofía,
Madrid

paths across her cheeks, in contrast to their more controlled formation
in figure 23. Her lashes are clusters of spiky leaves. Her bulbous,
enlarged nostrils are joined to form a snout. Picasso experimented with
rapidly scribbled patches of line on her cheeks, between her eyes, and
around her mouth, whose fleshy lips form a gaping hole containing
jagged teeth and a knifelike tongue.

A third weeping woman (fig. 25), drawn 27 May, is also
disheveled, the result of lines rapidly scribbled on virtually all her
features. Such hasty gestures indicate the certainty with which Picasso

Figure 25
Weeping Woman
27 May 1937
Pencil and gouache
on paper
9 x 11 ⅝ in.
(23 x 29.5 cm)
Museo Nacional Centro
de Arte Reina Sofía,
Madrid

executed these figures; he labored over the elements he had yet to finalize and rapidly sketched those with which he was less obsessed. Her eyes now come together on one side of her face, and her eyebrows are two prominent angles retraced several times. Her right ear is presented as two overlapping ovals on the side of her head, while another ear is visible at the top. A quickly executed series of teeth and the texture of her lips are the result of several looping strokes. Her tears both fall and rise, defying gravity, and her hair, as in the previous drawing, is a mass of scribbles. Evidently Picasso was considering the question of clothing: these three women wear, respectively, a dotted V-neck collar, a striped crew-neck shirt, and a checkered blouse.

The women's heads of 20 and 24 May (figs. 21, 23) and those of 24 and 27 May (figs. 24–25) indicate two degrees of emotional distress Picasso considered in developing the figure of the falling woman at the right of *Guernica*. He appears to have been willing to explore extreme states in his studies, but in the evolving mural he adopted relatively toned-down expressions for his figures. When his work on the mural was recorded on the 27th (fig. 26), the visage of the falling woman, like the face of the mother with dead child at the left side of the canvas, most closely resembled the 20 May drawing. Picasso once again altered the position of her arms, now resolutely having them point upward, with open hands desperately reaching for something to hold on to. Although he had considered replacing her with a weeping man and rapidly sketched one that day (fig. 27), he evidently rejected changing the figure's gender and retained the concept of two women framing the composition.

The following morning, 28 May, Picasso resumed sketching the mother and dead child. For the first time the mother weeps. In his first study of the day (fig. 28) he endowed her with the teeth of the rearing horse of 2 May (fig. 12). Her teardrop-shaped eyes are weighted by their pupils, with pronged eyelashes attached to each. She has no ears, and her nostrils are darts, a motif appearing here for the first time in the studies for *Guernica*. Her general configuration is essentially unchanged from the one already painted on the mural; what Picasso endeavored to resolve was her facial expression.

His approach in the second drawing of the day (fig. 29) was far more experimental. Here Picasso applied actual tangled hair to the mother's head. She now looks upward, her head tilted back at the same 90-degree angle that Picasso had used in the falling woman. This drawing is a marked rethinking of the entire left side of the composition, from the architecture (Picasso now considered placing a burning building there) to the woman's pose (it mirrors that of the fleeing woman at

Figure 26
Dora Maar
Guernica, state v
Photographed around
27 May 1937

Figure 27
Falling Man
27 May 1937
Pencil and gouache
on paper
9 x 11 ⁵/₈ in.
(23 x 29.5 cm)
Museo Nacional Centro
de Arte Reina Sofía,
Madrid

Figure 28
Mother with Dead Child
28 May 1937
Pencil, crayon, and
gouache on paper
9 x 11 ¾ in.
(23 x 30 cm)
Museo Nacional Centro
de Arte Reina Sofía,
Madrid

the canvas's lower right). The mother is now in a state of frenzy—and
for good reason. A lance runs prominently through the child's body, yet
the child, arm upraised and mouth open, appears to be still alive, though
barely. The scene is one of utter terror. The mother simultaneously
flees, shields, and reaches for help. Her tongue and teeth jut out of her
wide-open mouth; her eyes roll back in her head, while tears stream
from them.

  That Picasso elected not to incorporate such a violent image
into the mural is significant. Once more he chose the more restrained
approach, with suggestive but not blatant figures. He resolved to let
the figures' faces convey the emotion of the scene, believing that these
images, read in the aggregate, would effectively express his anti-Franco,
pro-republic message. He now devoted his energies to refining the

Figure 29
Mother with Dead Child
28 May 1937
Pencil, crayon, gouache,
and hair on paper
9 x 11 ³/₈ in.
(23 x 29 cm)
Museo Nacional Centro
de Arte Reina Sofía,
Madrid

motif. His color study of a weeping woman from the same day (fig. 30) is a compromise between the more restrained versions (figs. 21, 23, and 28) and the more radical solutions (figs. 24, 25, and 29) of the previous week. The scribbled hair last seen the day before (fig. 25) and the sprouting lashes first appearing on 24 May (fig. 24) adorn a head of simplified contour. There is an ear at the top of the face and another where the head meets the neck. Tears flow in long arcs downward along the cheeks; the comma-shaped nostrils seem to be tears of another sort. Picasso labored over the mouth, carefully drawing each tooth, describing

Figure 30
Weeping Woman
28 May 1937
Pencil, crayon, and gouache on paper
9 x 11 ⅝ in.
(23 x 29.5 cm)
Museo Nacional Centro de Arte Reina Sofia, Madrid

the upper and lower palates, and shaping the lips. These weathered lips
and rotten teeth are suggestive of the peasant population of Guernica;
they underscore the likely metaphorical relationship between Guernica's
inhabitants and the weeping women Picasso had planned for the mural.
The application of orange to the tears strangely animates the face, in a
macabre reference to the "made-up" ladies of Paris—initially seen in the
artist-and-model studies—that Picasso had eliminated from his mono-
chromatic mural.

Picasso did not work during the last weekend of May. Most
likely he spent part of his time visiting Walter and their daughter Maya
at Ambroise Vollard's house in Tremblay-sur-Mauldre.[18] A single sheet
drawn the following Monday, 31 May (fig. 31), contains several images.
A weeping head is superimposed on a burning building and a large
hand; the head is crossed by a swath of yellow flame or smoke emanating
from the building. The juxtaposition suggests that this study, like the
28 May sketches, is related to the falling woman. The reappearance of the
burning building demonstrates that a suggestion of the devastation that
prompted the women's weeping was essential to Picasso's underlying
concept. The eyes have become thickly outlined mollusks encircled in
blue; the lashes still sprout in clusters, but the eyebrows look like stalks
of wheat. The nostrils are darts again, now encircled. We see every
tooth and its root. The woman has several strands of tentaclelike hair
at the nape of her neck in addition to thin hairs elsewhere. Her tears
consist of thin, orange rivulets; the drops at the ends are echoed by thick,
vertical streaks of blue and green. The increased intricacy of this drawing
indicates that Picasso was by now fully immersed in the question of how
best to express grief and despair. He was actively articulating each feature
in a manner previously unexplored, and his addition of color now cast
the entire head in an eerie glow.

Despite these explorations, however, the painted portions of
the mural itself had not changed significantly by the time it was photographed around 1 June. He added several collage elements of wallpaper,
but the figures remained unchanged.[19] It is likely that Picasso visited the
pavilion sometime during the first week of June, and that he assessed the

Figure 31
Weeping Woman
31 May 1937
Pencil, crayon, and
gouache on paper
9 x 11 ⅝ in.
(23 x 29.5 cm)
Museo Nacional Centro
de Arte Reina Sofía,
Madrid

location and environmental situation of the mural. José Lluis Sert, one of the pavilion's architects, probably visited Picasso in his Grands Augustins studio at this time to ascertain his progress; there was considerable concern among the pavilion's organizers that the mural would not be ready in time for the opening.[20]

Though Picasso would remove the pieces of wallpaper from the canvas in the next several days, the painting was very close to its final form. Nevertheless, he continued to make sketches related to the weeping woman and the dead warrior. Three extraordinary weeping heads date from 3 June. One (fig. 32) is a slightly modified version of figure 31. Extraneous detail is eliminated and individual features are sharpened. The eyes are still mollusks, but their lashes are minimal; the eyebrows are clearly defined stalks of wheat. Tears now stream only from tear ducts, marked by stars. The nostrils are darts transformed into elongated hearts with halos. The mouth is less crowded, though there are far too many teeth lined up along the lower palate and six large teeth along the upper. The tongue is an unadorned triangle; the lips are modeled with six short curving lines. The ear is now crescent-shaped, and its auditory function is conveyed by the diverging lines emanating from it. The hair consists solely of tentacles. Patches of color enliven the forms but do not add substantive detail.

In Picasso's second pass at the theme that day (fig. 33) planes of blue, red, and yellow intersect on the face, and the head, topped by small, triangular flames, is set in front of a field of green. This woman has long, thick lashes, and her tears amplify the contours of her face. Her ear is hollow, like the mouth of a horn. Her teeth are neatly aligned, and her tongue is now richly textured. Picasso in fact reversed the placement of the textures on the upper surface of the tongue so that what is most visible on the tip of an actual tongue is, on the tongue of this woman, furthest from the tip.[21] Picasso's attention to such minute anatomical detail indicates how very thorough was his experimentation with these figures. The third drawing of the day (fig. 34) is the most chaotic. The tentacular hairs are falling all over. The tears run in serpentine patterns along her ill-defined cheek. The precise contour of

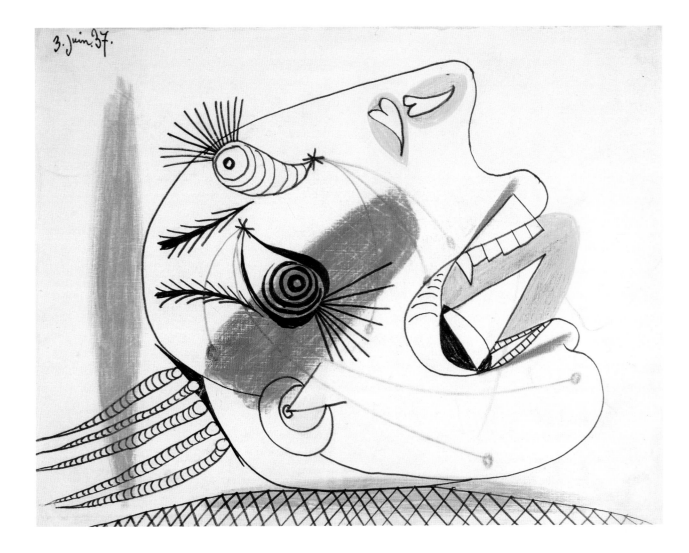

Figure 32
Weeping Woman
3 June 1937
Pencil, crayon, and
gouache on paper
9 x 11 ⅝ in.
(23 x 29.5 cm)
Museo Nacional Centro
de Arte Reina Sofía,
Madrid

this head is difficult to discern where it disappears along the hairline. Her mollusk eyes now contain several concentric circles, and lashes extend from them like dangling wires. The teeth have multiplied, and the wedge of the tongue has been softened. Her ear has become a frame with sound waves visualized inside it.

Beginning with the 31 May drawing (fig. 31), his renderings of the weeping women depart from previous versions. They are more readable as monstrous masks than as expressive faces. Picasso did not use any of them in *Guernica*. The very fact that he was preoccupied with them—indeed with nothing but them—in the closing days of completing the mural suggests that he was considering last-minute options to alter aspects of the painting. With the aid of sketches made during the week of 31 May he continued to make changes to the fallen warrior and to other small areas, but essentially he was concluding his work. Maar's final

photograph prior to the completion of the canvas was taken around 4 June, and the painting was delivered to the pavilion a week or so later.

"In the panel on which I am working, which I shall call *Guernica*," wrote Picasso, "and in all my recent works of art, I clearly express my abhorrence of the military caste which has sunk Spain in an ocean of pain and death."[22] This ocean of pain and death consumed him. He continued to consider alterations throughout the day that the canvas departed his studio. Although the mural arrived at the pavilion in mid-June, the architects thought Picasso would continue to work on it until the inauguration on 12 July, which he apparently did not. Picasso told Sert: "I don't know when I will finish it. Maybe never. You had better come and take it whenever you need it."[23]

"It was necessary for the pictorial expression to be horrible, for the outlines to weep, for the discolored color to be one of sadness,

Figure 33
Weeping Woman
3 June 1937
Pencil, crayon, and gouache on paper
9 ¼ x 11 ½ in.
(23.5 x 29.2 cm)
Museo Nacional Centro de Arte Reina Sofía, Madrid

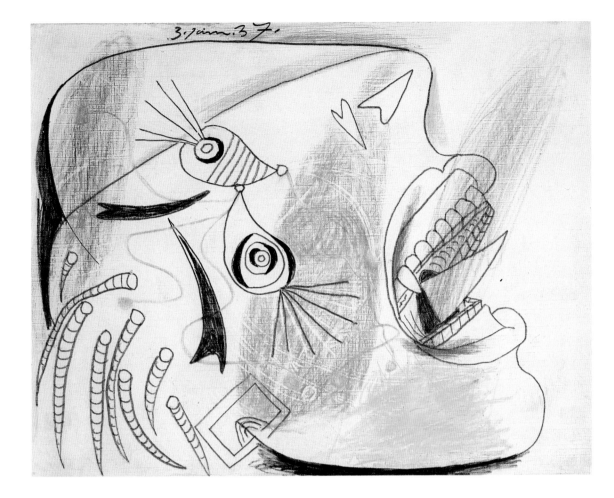

Figure 34

Weeping Woman

3 June 1937

Pencil, crayon, and

gouache on paper

9 x 11 ⅝ in.

(23 x 29.5 cm)

Museo Nacional Centro

de Arte Reina Sofía,

Madrid

for the whole to be a penetrating clamor—tenacious, strident, and eternal," observed Jaime Sabartès, Picasso's secretary and confidant.[24] Picasso's absorption in each individual feature of the women's faces and his repeated reworking of those features was the key to his effort to attain this clamor. Films made of Picasso's *Guernica* contain footage where the camera creeps along the surface of the canvas, slowly taking in every minute detail and nuance.[25] This was Picasso's desired effect, and his studies attest to his methodical search for the most suitable motif for each figure. Picasso unleashed his *Guernica* (fig. 35) for the world to share in the town's—and the artist's—tragedy. With the painting's departure from his studio Picasso abandoned for a time the themes of the mother with dead child and the fallen warrior. The one motif he could not relinquish was that of the weeping woman. Her visage haunted him. He drew her frequently, almost obsessively, for the next several months. She was the metaphor for his own private agonies.

Figure 35

(overleaf)

Guernica

May/June 1937

Oil on canvas

137 ⅜ x 305 ⅞ in.

(349 x 777 cm)

Museo Nacional Centro

de Arte Reina Sofía,

Madrid. On permanent

loan from the Prado

Museum

Notes

1. Michel Leiris, "Faire-part," *Cahiers d'art* 12, nos. 4–5 (1937): 128. Trans. in Oppler 1988, 210.

2. *Dream and Lie of Franco* was first published, with all states of the prints, in *Cahiers d'art*; see Picasso 1937, 37–50. See the particularly good analyses in Failing 1977, 55–64; and Spies 1988, 45–62.

3. *"...espadas de pulpos de mal agüero estropajo de pelos de coronillas de pie en medio de la sartén..."* The text, though written in Spanish, first appeared in *Cahiers d'art* in French. Picasso 1989, 166.

4. *"...productos de belleza del carro de la basura— rapto de las meninas en lágrimas y en lagrimones— al hombro el ataúd relleno de chorizos y de bocas... farol de piojos donde está el perro nudo de ratas y escondrijo del palacio de trapos viejos—las banderas que fríen en la sartén se retuercen en el negro de la salsa de la tinta derramada en las gotas de sangre que lo fusilan..."* Ibid.

5. *"...gritos de niños gritos de mujeres gritos de pájaros gritos de flores gritos de maderas y de piedras gritos de ladrillos gritos de muebles de camas de sillas de cortinas de cazuelas de gatos y de papeles gritos de olores que se arañan gritos de humo picando en el morrillo de los gritos que cuecen en el caldero y de la lluvia de pájaros que inunda el mar..."* Ibid.

6. *"rage de dents aux yeux du soleil pique—pique rage du soleil de dents aux yeux—yeux aux dents pique du soleil de rage du soleil pique yeux aux dents de rage aux dents—du soleil pique de rage yeux fleur..."* Ibid., 156.

7. Joan Miró, *Selected Writings and Interviews*, ed. Margit Rowell, trans. by Paul Auster and Patricia Mathews (Boston: G.K. Hall, 1986): 141. This is from Miró's notebook of poems, 1936–39 (Fundació Joan Miró, Barcelona).

8. In January 1937 José Gaos (general commissioner of the Spanish Pavilion), the poet Louis Aragon, Max Aub (cultural delegate at the Spanish Embassy in Paris), and the architect José Lluis Sert visited Picasso at his apartment on the rue La Boëtie and asked him to paint a mural for the pavilion. For the details of the commission see Sert, typescript of statement in the symposium on *Guernica* at The Museum of Modern Art, 25 November 1947, 6–12 (Museum of Modern Art Library, New York); also Freedberg 1986.

9. He drew these while visiting Marie-Thérèse Walter and their daughter, Maya, at Tremblay-sur-Mauldre. For a detailed discussion of these works, see Ullman 1986A, 4–26; Chipp 1988A, 58–69; and 1988B, 62–67.

10. In Seckler 1945, 7. There has been considerable debate in the *Guernica* literature over the associations of the bull and the horse. For example Blunt 1969, 14, cites the Seckler interview, where Picasso identifies the horse with the people and the bull with the forces of brutality and darkness. Larrea 1947, 33, 36–7, rejects this view and considers the bull to be the embodiment of Picasso, not only in this but in other quasi-autobiographical pictures of the 1930s; the horse is a woman "who played an exceptionally important part in his life." He also suggests that in *Guernica* the horse represents Spanish nationalism and the bull is a symbol of the Spanish people.

11. Several volumes reproduce all of Picasso's preparatory studies for *Guernica*: Larrea 1947; Arnheim 1962; Zervos 1932–78, vol. 9; Russell 1980; Chipp 1988A; and Oppler 1988. Arnheim and Oppler reproduce as well all of the postscripts related to *Guernica*. I am especially indebted to Chipp's thoughtful and thorough study of *Guernica*.

12. For example, in *Le Figaro*, 3 May; *L'Humanité*, 5, 7, 9, and 14 May; *L'Illustration*, 8 May; and *Paris-Soir*, 8 May.

For a thorough discussion of Picasso's awareness of the events unfolding in Guernica, see Tuchman 1983, 44–51; and especially Chipp 1988A, 38–43, 93. For excellent documentation of the dissemination of the news from Guernica, see Southworth 1977. My account has benefited from these three sources.

13. George L. Steer, "The Tragedy of Guernica," *The Times* (London) 28 April 1937; trans. and published in *L'Humanité* (Paris) 29 April 1937; reprinted in Oppler 1988, 160–63.

14. *L'Humanité,* 30 April/1 May 1937 (weekend edition); trans. in Chipp 1988A, 40–41.

15. I am indebted to William S. Lieberman for suggesting the stage-set quality of Picasso's composition for *Guernica*.

16. This is evident in Dora Maar's "State II" (c. 13 May) and "State III" (c. 16–19 May) photographs of the canvas; reproduced in Chipp 1988A, 117, 121 (figs. 7.13 and 7.20).

17. See Maar's "State II (det.)" and "State IIA" photographs, ibid., 119 (figs. 7.18 and 7.19).

18. Roland Penrose described these as weekly visits; see Penrose 1981A, 302.

19. Sert stated in 1947 that he saw the painting in the studio several weeks after Picasso had begun it, at which time it had wallpaper on it. Sert, typescript, 8; see note 8.

20. "Until the last moment everyone was doubtful that we would get the mural in time for the opening." Sert, unpublished letter of 29 November 1980 to Dominique Bozo, director of the Musée Picasso, Paris (Archives of the Musée Picasso, Paris)

21. He has reversed the placement of the median lingual suicus, the lingual papillae, and the lingual tonsil.

22. Picasso, "Picasso's Statement," in *The Springfield Republican* (18 July 1937): 21; repr. in Picasso 1972, 143. The statement was probably written in May or early June.

23. Sert, typescript, 9; see note 8.

24. Sabartès, cited in Janet Flanner, "The Surprise of the Century, II," *The New Yorker*, 16 March 1957, 39.

25. Robert Flaherty's unfinished film on the painting, made in cooperation with The Museum of Modern Art, New York, in 1949, contains this sort of footage. I am grateful to William S. Lieberman, who wrote the never-recorded script, for alerting me to the film's existence in The Museum of Modern Art's Film Study Archive.

26 octobre 37.

CHAPTER III

"...by virtue of what cold

"What do you think an artist is? An imbecile who only has eyes if he's a painter, ears if he's a musician, or a lyre in every chamber of his heart if he's a poet or even, if he's a boxer, only some muscles? Quite the contrary, he is at the same time a political being constantly alert to the horrifying, passionate or pleasing events in the world, shaping himself completely in their image. How is it possible to be uninterested in other men and by virtue of what cold nonchalance can you detach yourself from a life that they supply so copiously? No, painting is not made to decorate apartments. It's an offensive and defensive weapon against the enemy."

—Pablo Picasso, writing at the end of the Occupation of France, 1945[1]

"*I*n the autumn of the year in which *Guernica* had been painted," wrote the artist and critic Roland Penrose,

I paid Picasso a visit one morning with Paul Eluard. When he showed us into his studio we were both astonished at the captivating power of a small newly painted canvas placed on an easel as though he were still at work on it. The Woman Weeping [Penrose is referring to Weeping Woman, **fig. 83***] had been finished on the day after his fifty-sixth birthday in October 1937. It came as a postscript to the great mural and contained an account of the agony caused by fascist aggression on humanity. The sombre monochrome of* Guernica *had given place to brilliant contrasts of red, blue, green, and yellow in a highly disconcerting way. It was as though this girl, seen in profile but with both the dark passionate eyes of Dora Maar, dressed as for a fête, had found herself suddenly faced by heartrending disaster. For a while the impact of this small brilliant canvas left us speechless and after a few enthusiastic exclamations I heard myself say to Picasso "Oh! may I buy that from you?" and heard in a daze his answer "And why not?" There followed the exchange of a cheque for £250 for one of the master- pieces of this century.*[2]

Why did Picasso remain obsessed with the weeping women well after he had accomplished the herculean feat of painting *Guernica*? What was it about this motif that, unlike the warrior, the bull, and the horse, pre- occupied the artist for six additional months?

On one level the weeping woman represented the victims of Guernica. She was the grieving mother, the terrified peasant, the stunned survivor. She was witness to bloodshed and unspeakable horrors. When Picasso filled in the fifteenth panel of his *Dream and Lie of Franco* on 7 June with the head of a weeping woman (fig. 4), he was making clear his own passionate opposition to Franco and also telling the world that the ordinary person was watching and suffering. By inserting the weeping woman into what was essentially an anti-Franco handbill, Picasso had symbolized Franco's victims, who were also witnesses. The upturned head he created combines elements from his images of 27, 28, and 31 May and the three heads of 3 June (figs. 27–34). Her pose loosely

Page 66: detail
Sheet of Studies: Tears
(Figure 80)

Figure 36
Weeping Woman
8 June 1937
Pencil and gouache
on paper
11 ³/₈ x 9 in.
(29 x 23 cm)
Museo Nacional Centro
de Arte Reina Sofía,
Madrid

resembles that of the falling woman in *Guernica*, but tears transform her face into a wrenching and far more intense portrait of pathos. Her mass of tangled hair, the pattern of the tears crisscrossing her cheek, her wide-open mouth (note the lack of a prominent tongue), and her lash-studded eyes all serve to make her a concentrated block of raw emotions.

The heads of 31 May and 3 June and the etched head in *Dream and Lie of Franco* of 7 June are as masklike as Picasso's weeping figures get. On 8 June Picasso began to restore human features to them. The differences are small but significant. The two heads of that day sit comfortably on their necks. Picasso quickly drew the essential features of one (fig. 36): a few curves form the contours of the face. The teardrop-shaped eyes have hairlike lashes for the first time. Teardrops hang from

the ends of the crisp, fine lines that trace their passage. The nostrils are darts within circles, the single ear is formed by two concentric ovals with a hole, and the lips are soft, fleshy flaps harboring a rounded tongue. Later that day Picasso resketched—he may have even traced— the same image (fig. 37) and then enhanced it, adding more hair, drawing lines on the brow, thickening the eyebrows, filling in the area around the mouth and chin, and changing the pattern of tears on the cheeks. He returned to the same profile again nearly one week later

Figure 37
Weeping Woman
8 June 1937
Pencil, crayon, and
gouache on paper
11 ⅜ x 9 in.
(29 x 23 cm)
Museo Nacional Centro
de Arte Reina Sofía,
Madrid

Figure 38

Weeping Woman

13 June 1937

Pencil, crayon, and

gouache on paper

11 ³⁄₈ x 9 in.

(29 x 23 cm)

Museo Nacional Centro

de Arte Reina Sofía,

Madrid

(fig. 38), eliminating some of the details he had added on 8 June and subtly altering others. He reduced the number of fine lines modeling the face, removed the circles around the nostrils, colored the lips and tongue, and scribbled inside the eye sockets, calling greater attention to the teardrop-shaped eyes. The ear is upright, nestled in a cascade of wavy, shoulder-length hair.

These three heads—the last he made in this format—were all drawn on the same sketchbook paper that Picasso had used while

fandango de lechuzas escabeche de espadas de pulpos de mal agüero
estropajo de pelos de coronillas de pié en medio de la sartén en
pelotas — puesto sobre el encuentro del sorbete de bacalao
frito en la sarna de su corazón de cabestro — la boca llena de
la jalea de chinches de sus palabras — cascabeles del plato
de caracoles trenzando tripas — menique en erección ni uva
ni prueba — comedia del arte de mal tejer y teñir nubes
— productos de belleza del carro de la papara — rapto de las meninas
en lágrimas y sen lagrimones — al hombro el ataud relleno de chorizos
y de boca — la rabia retorciendo el dibujo de la sombra que le azota los
dientes clavados en la arena y el caballo abierto de par en par
al sol que lo lee á las moscas que hilvanan á las niñas de la
red llena de boquerones el cohete de azucenas — farol de piojos
donde esta el perro nudo de ratas y escondrijo del palacio de trapos
viejos las banderas que fríen en la sartén se retuercen en el negro
de la salsa de la tinta derramada en las gotas de jamuse que lo pasitan
— la calle sube á las nubes atada por los pies al mar de pena y que pudre
sus entrañas y el reloj que la cubre cuenta, baila loco de pena del suelo
la cañas de pescar y althigui althigui del entierro de primera del carro de
mudanza — las alas rotas rodando sobre la tela de arena del pan seco y
agua clara de la paella de azúcar y terciopelo que pinta el latigazo en
sus mejillas — la luz se tapa los ojos delante del espejo que hace
el mono y el trozo de turrón de las llamas se muerde los labios
de la herida — gritos de niños gritos de mujeres gritos de pájaros
gritos de flores gritos de maderas y de piedras gritos de ladrillos gritos de
muebles de camas de sillas de cortinas de cazuelas de gatos y de papeles
gritos de olores que se arañan gritos de humo picando en el morrillo
de los gritos que cuecen en el caldero y de la lluvia de pájaros
que inunda el mar que roe el hueso y se rompe los dientes
mordiendo el algodón que el sol lebrina en el plato
que el bolsón y la bolsa esconden en la huella que el pié
deja en la roca —

Figure 39
Manuscript for
Dream and Lie of Franco
15-18 June 1937, state II
Pencil and crayon on
paper
21 ⅝ x 14 ½ in.
(55.5 x 37 cm)
Donation Yvonne and
Christian Zervos,
Vézelay, France

preparing *Guernica*, so they were no doubt a continuation of his practice of preparing studies in his sketchbook, even after the mural was completed. He devoted several days of the following week to writing the text for *Dream and Lie of Franco*. It was an intuitive text, produced in one draft without revisions. As we have already seen, it included several references to cries, but it also contained sordid stream-of-consciousness summations of the realities of war: "...the fury twisting the shape of the shadow that whips it the teeth armed with nails in the sand and the horse wide open to the sun that reads him to the flies that they string to the knots of the net full of anchovies the missile of lilies."[3] When he had completed his text Picasso lightly colored it with hues of purple, blue, and yellow (fig. 39). At the bottom he hastily drew, in several colors, the head of a reclining woman; tears cascade from her eyes through her hair.

On 26 June Picasso returned to the weeping woman motif and drew and painted it instead on canvas (fig. 40), taking elements from several of the preparatory drawings and combining them. This slightly rounder head tilts back more than the ones of 8 June (figs. 36–37) and 13 June (fig. 38), but the features are essentially the same. The furrowed brow reappears, and the number of tears has increased; the mouth is open wide, as if in the midst of a scream. The painting is a more agonized version of the drawings; it is also twice their size. The larger format is a typical portrait scale for Picasso; his numerous bust-length canvases are of similar dimensions.

Figure 40
Weeping Woman
26 June 1937
Pencil, crayon,
and oil on canvas
21 ⅝ x 18 ⅛ in.
(55 x 46 cm)
Museo Nacional Centro
de Arte Reina Sofía,
Madrid

Figure 41
Weeping Woman
19 June 1937
Pencil and gouache
on board
4 ½ x 3 ½ in.
(11.5 x 9 cm)
Museo Nacional Centro
de Arte Reina Sofía,
Madrid

It is a standard French canvas format—10F, or 55 x 46 cm.—implying that Picasso, who would have conceived of selling this picture (unlike his sketchbook sheets), had brought the weeping woman motif to some state of resolution.

In fact he was concurrently completing a number of variants on this theme. He returned briefly to the subject of the mother with her dead child. A study on a small board (fig. 41) of an upturned head combines the facial features of the more recent weeping women with the pose of the figure on the left side of *Guernica*.[4] Once again the window at the left is an indication that Picasso was never quite certain about the resolution of the left side of the painting, as he continued to rehash this element of the composition. Light from the window illuminates the face and makes its pain all the more apparent. The painted version executed on 22 June (fig. 42) makes clear his desire to rethink the arrangement of the mother and child pair. Their appearance—at first glance—suggests a scene of maternal intimacy. Picasso's obsession with the elongated line of the neck, characteristic of the fleeing figure in the mural, has an additional compositional function here: it provides a space in which the head of the child can nestle. The woman's hands are brought close to her face as she cradles the child. Her face is a simplified version of the drawn heads of 28 May, 31 May, and 3 June (figs. 28–34), but her expression evokes the genuine horror of a mother's despair.

For the next two months Picasso abandoned the mother-and-dead-child theme and returned to his preoccupation with the weeping woman. He created a drawing and two paintings of her on 22 June (figs. 43–45).[5] Her head is in profile, but it is angled in a downward direction so that her grief seems to be less exposed and more internalized than in Picasso's previous depictions of her. For the first time she holds a hand-

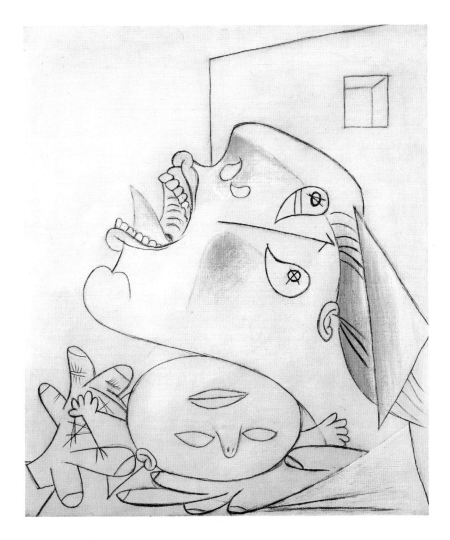

Figure 42
Woman with Dead Child
22 June 1937
Pencil, crayon,
and oil on canvas
21 ⁵⁄₈ x 18 ¹⁄₈ in.
(55 x 46 cm)
Museo Nacional Centro
de Arte Reina Sofía,
Madrid

kerchief, a new visual element for Picasso. This appears as a mound of cloth in loose folds, held by hands like giant blades; two elongated fingers have sharp nails, a reference perhaps to Dora Maar, renowned for her long, tapered fingernails. Picasso's addition of these elements— the scissorlike hands, the wad of cloth—suggests that he felt a need to underscore the woman's grief (symbolized by the handkerchief) and rage (conveyed by the scissor-hands) through the use of such attributes and props.

Picasso's interest in equipping his figures with handkerchiefs found an echo in his use of another sort of tissue. As *Guernica* was near-

Figure 43
*Weeping Woman
with Handkerchief*
22 June 1937
Oil on canvas
21 ⁵⁄₈ x 18 ¹⁄₈ in.
(55 x 46 cm)
Museo Nacional Centro
de Arte Reina Sofía,
Madrid

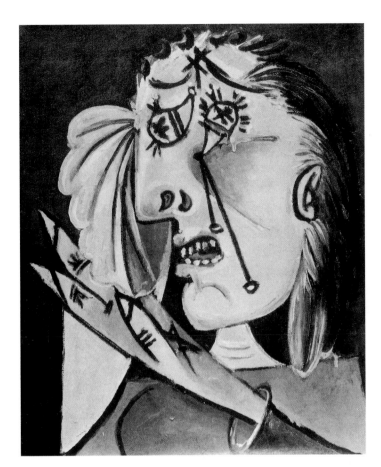

Figure 44

*Weeping Woman
with Handkerchief*

22 June 1937

Oil on canvas

21 ⁵/₈ x 18 ¹/₈ in.

(55 x 46 cm)

Private collection

ing completion, Henry Moore accompanied Roland Penrose on a visit
to Picasso. Moore recalled:

*You know the woman who comes running out of the little cabin on the right with
one hand held in front of her? Well, Picasso told us that there was something
missing there, and he went and fetched a roll of paper and stuck it in the
woman's hand, as much as to say that she'd been caught in the bathroom when
the bombs came.*[6]

Penrose recalled the occasion as well:

*Picasso silently disappeared and returned with a long piece of toilet paper, which
he pinned to the hand of the woman on the right of the composition, who runs*

Figure 45

*Weeping Woman
with Handkerchief*

22 June 1937

Pencil and gouache
on paper

25 ¹/₄ x 19 ¹/₂ in.

(64 x 49.5 cm)

Private collection,
France

June to December 1937

77

into the scene terrified and yet curious to know what is happening. As though she had been disturbed at a critical moment her bottom is bare and her alarm too great to notice it. "There," said Picasso, "that leaves no doubt about the commonest and most primitive effect of fear." [7]

Figure 46
*Woman Crowned
with Flowers*
24 June 1937
Oil on canvas
18 x 13 in.
(45.7 x 33 cm)
Private collection

His use of these and other accouterments had greater personal significance than either Moore or Penrose realized at the time. One of his earliest and most vivid memories of kerchiefs dated from the Málaga earthquake of 1884. He was three years old. His mother was at the end of her pregnancy with his sister Lola when the earthquake struck. "My mother was wearing a kerchief on her head. I had never seen her like that," he told his friend and assistant Sabartès. "My father grabbed his cape from the rack, threw it over himself, picked me up in his arms, and wrapped me in its folds leaving only my head exposed." [8]

Moore and Penrose's visit probably took place around 1 June. Picasso at that time was experimenting with collaged additions— including wallpaper—to *Guernica*; the toilet paper, like the wallpaper, was soon removed. Nevertheless the idea of the applied element stuck, and Picasso saw its potential, in the form of the handkerchief, as the weeping women developed.

The basic shape of the heads of 22 June (figs. 43–45) was retained by Picasso when he painted, for the first time since he had begun the *Guernica* studies, an altogether different subject. His portrait of Marie-Thérèse Walter crowned with flowers (fig. 46) has a nearly identical profile. In virtually all of the weeping women, as in the numerous portraits of Walter, the eyes are shown frontally, while the nose and mouth are seen from the side. The flowered crown is Walter's accouterment, as the handkerchief is the weeping woman's. This is not the first or last time Picasso would paint her with the crown, but here she is distinctly downcast. Her lids are half closed, her gaze seems to be lowered.[9] While the flowers speak of her youth and vitality, her eyes possess a wisdom far beyond her years.

Two days later, on 26 June, Picasso brought to completion his concept of the Spanish weeping woman (fig. 47). She holds a handker-

Figure 47

*Weeping Woman
with Handkerchief*
26 June 1937
Oil on canvas
21 ⁵/₈ x 18 ¹/₈ in.
(54.9 x 46 cm)
Los Angeles County
Museum of Art,
Gift of Mr. and Mrs.
Thomas Mitchell

chief and wears a plaid mantilla, which frames her reddish hair. One hand is silhouetted against her chest. The white gauze handkerchief is crumpled into a shapeless mass. She cries into it, but her tears fall all over her face. Tear ducts appear on the outer edges of her eyes, which are filled with daubs of black paint and edged with clumps of lashes. Running through the furrows in her brow is a crease that splits her face down the middle. Her cheeks are flushed; her nose, red. The elements of the composition interlock perfectly. The face, the handkerchief, and the hand holding it are seamlessly enmeshed to make her the emblem of despair. Yet crowned with the traditional matronly mantilla, she is also the embodiment of Spanish womanhood.

By the time this painting was completed *Guernica* had been installed in the Spanish pavilion.[10] It galvanized the presentation of the horrors of the civil war then raging in Spain. At the entrance to the pavilion was Julio González's *Montserrat*, a life-size iron sculpture of a woman holding a child on her shoulder. In addition to Picasso's mural a fountain by Alexander Calder, *Spanish Mercury from Almadén,* stood in the foyer. Opposite the painting was a monumental photograph of the poet Federico García Lorca, assassinated by Franco's forces in Grenada one year earlier. Adjacent to the foyer was an auditorium where Luis Buñuel organized screenings of films documenting the war by internationally known writers and filmmakers. Among them were Buñuel's *Madrid '36*, John Dos Passos and Archibald MacLeish's *Spain in Flames*, Joris Ivens and Ernest Hemingway's *Spanish Earth*, Paul Strand's *The Heart of Spain*, and Tristan Tzara's *Madrid—Verdun of Democracy.* These films graphically presented the devastation of the country and the suffering of the Spanish people. Miró's eighteen-foot-high mural *The Reaper* (fig. 48) hung above the steps to the pavilion's lower level. This painting (now lost) depicts a massive, bust-length head holding a sickle in one hand and reaching upward with the other. Whether the reaper is male or female is ambiguous, though the jagged teeth and jellyfishlike eye resemble those used by Picasso in the weeping women.

The lower level of the pavilion featured photomurals. Some detailed the economic and cultural life of Spain under the republican

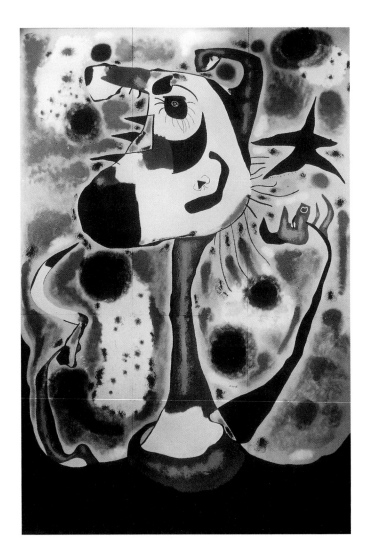

Figure 48
Joan Miró
The Reaper
1937
Mural on celotex
216 ½ x 142 ⅞ in.
(550 x 363 cm)
Now lost

government; others evoked the experiences of the Spanish people during
wartime. One of these featured two large photographs of refugee children, another (fig. 49) depicted casualties of the fighting. Paul Eluard's
poem "The Victory of Guernica" was printed on a wall adjacent to a
photograph of the city's remains:

1

High life in hovels
In mines and in fields

2

Faces staunch in the fire staunch in the cold
Against denials the night insults blows

3

Faces always staunch

Here is the void staring at you

Your death shall be an example

4

Death heart overturned

5

They made you pray for bread

Sky earth water sleep

And the poverty

Of your life

Figure 49
Photomural in the
Spanish pavilion of the
International Exposition
of Arts and Techniques
in Modern Life, Paris,
1937; photographed by
François Kollar

6

They said they wanted agreement

They checked the strong sentenced the mad

Gave alms divided a farthing

They greeted every corpse

They overwhelmed each other with politeness

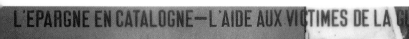

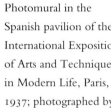

7

They insist they exaggerate they are not of our world

8

The women the children have the same treasure
Of green leaves of spring and of pure milk
And of endurance
In their pure eyes

9

The women the children have the same treasure
In their eyes
The men defend it as best they can

10

The women the children have the same red roses
In their eyes
All show their blood

11

The fear and the courage of living and of dying
Death so hard and so easy

12

Men for whom this treasure was extolled
Men for whom this treasure was spoiled

13

Real men for whom despair
Feeds the devouring fire of hope
Let us open together the last bud of the future

14

Pariahs
Death earth and the vileness of our enemies
Have the monotonous color of our night
The day will be ours [11]

Figure 50
Ricardo Boix Oviedo
*Dream of the Sadness
of Spain*
1937
Stone
84 ¼ x 50 x 9 ⅛ in.
(214 x 127 x 22 cm)
Museu Nacional d'Art de
Catalunya, Barcelona

On the second floor were other contemporary works of Spanish art,[12] clearly chosen with the pavilion's theme in mind. Depictions of women dominated; among the most compelling were those of women as refugees or victims. Ricardo Boix Oviedo's massive stone relief *Dream of the Sadness of Spain* (fig. 50) used the emblem of a mother tightly clutching her child to symbolize the Spanish tragedy, much as Picasso had done. José García Narezo's *The Woman Who Went Crazy from the Crimes She Witnessed* (fig. 51), from a series of drawings titled *War and Crime*, features the classically inspired head of a woman. One large tear streams down her cheek. She is framed by the tiny heads of other female witnesses of the destruction erupting around them. Clearly Picasso's preoccupation with the weeping woman motif was shared by other Spanish artists; the reverence for women, particularly mothers, in devoutly Catholic Spain, made them a particularly sympathetic motif in a forum, like the pavilion, designed to sway viewers' passions.

Picasso must have appreciated the pavilion's hard-hitting and heartrending propaganda. He was already anti-Franco and prorepublican; his *Dream and Lie of Franco* was a clear indication of this. Both full prints and postcards of individual frames were sold at the pavilion, along with Miró's poster *Help Spain*, to benefit the Spanish republican forces. The forceful depictions of victimized women and children in the exhibition had a strong impact on artists as well as ordinary citizens. Artist Amédée Ozenfant toured the pavilion and recorded his observations:

Sunday. *I am writing at a little table in the Catalan café of the Spanish Pavilion. Sorrowful. The exhibition of Spanish sorrow. Beneath a poignant photograph of orphans one reads: "Their parents were all they had had in the world ...and suffering has made their expression as profound as that of grown men...."*

La mujer que se volvió loca
6 por los crímenes que presenció

Figure 51

José García Narezo
*The Woman Who Went
Crazy from the Crimes
She Witnessed* (from the
series *War and Crime*)
1937
Pen and watercolor
on paper
10 ⅞ x 8 ¼ in.
(27.5 x 20.8 cm)
Museu Nacional d'Art
de Catalunya, Barcelona

*A well-dressed lady goes past my table, she's come down from the
second floor where there are exhibitions of Spanish war photographs: one sees
children massacred by Christians and Franco's Moors. The woman says to her
daughter:"That's all terrifying! It sends shivers down my spine as if I had a
spider running down my neck." She looks at* Guernica *and says to her child:
"I don't understand what is going on there, but it makes me feel awful. It's
strange, it really makes me feel as if I were being chopped to pieces. Come on,
let's go. War is a terrible thing! Poor Spain."And dragging her kid by the hand,
she goes off, uncertain, into the crowd.*[13]

Picasso's mural was difficult for artists, let alone laymen, to
comprehend. Its symbols were complex; its vast scale overwhelming. Its
individual motifs, on the other hand, were more accessible, since they
focused on individual responses to the tragedy of war. Picasso's reaction,
as a viewer at the pavilion, must have been especially acute. His family
and his roots were in Spain, yet he was helpless to take direct action
(even if he were so inclined) while in Paris.[14] In addition Picasso, director in absentia of the Museo del Prado since autumn 1936, was acutely
aware of the Spanish artistic heritage, the best of which was housed at
the Prado. It was now under direct threat due to the nationalist forces'
bombing of the museum, which had severely damaged parts of it, necessitating the secret evacuation of paintings.

Seen collectively, the works of art exhibited in the Spanish
pavilion were a modern analogue of Francisco Goya's 1820 *Disasters of
War*.[15] These widely disseminated etchings chronicled the French inva-
sion of Spain between 1808 and 1814. The eighty-five plates are among
the most graphic depictions ever made of war's cruel effects on an innocent populace. Goya's influence on Picasso was considerable; several of
the motifs in *Guernica* may be traced to individual prints in the series.[16]
One of the most wrenching images is number 62, *The Beds of the Dead*
(fig. 52), with its cloaked, kneeling, weeping woman. Picasso, particularly
in the wake of walking through the Spanish pavilion, was especially
attuned to Goya's mastery of such evocative single images.

Figure 52

Francisco Goya

The Beds of the Dead

1820

(No. 62 from

The Disasters of War)

Engraving

5 ⅞ x 7 ⅜ in.

(14.8 x 18.6 cm)

The Metropolitan

Museum of Art, New

York. Purchase, Rogers

Fund and Jacob H. Schiff

Bequest, 1922

Guernica, on the other hand, was a cacophony of motifs. In its complexity lies its genius as well as its difficulty. There was no accompanying explanatory text when it was shown in Paris and no catalogue to aid the interested viewer. When the painting left Paris and traveled, first to London (in October 1938) and then to the United States (beginning in May 1939), Picasso decided (probably in consultation with Roland Penrose) to send along sixty of its preparatory studies (all of which are now housed, along with *Guernica*, at the Museo Nacional Centro de arte Reina Sofia.)[17] On the announcement of its first London showing at the New Burlington Galleries the 26 June canvas *Weeping Woman*—not *Guernica* —was reproduced (fig. 53), suggesting that Picasso and Penrose considered the studies and the mural to be equally important and compelling.

Picasso in effect was editing and packaging his work, promoting the message of his mural as clearly and articulately as he possibly could. In this sense his efforts parallel those of Sergei Eisenstein, who divided his film *Potemkin* into six discrete sections to clarify the action. Picasso certainly saw this film; it had debuted in Paris in November

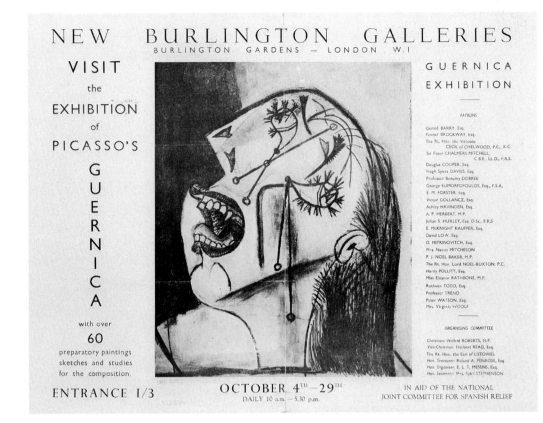

NEW BURLINGTON GALLERIES
BURLINGTON GARDENS — LONDON W.1

VISIT
the
EXHIBITION
of
PICASSO'S
GUERNICA
with over
60
preparatory paintings
sketches and studies
for the composition.
ENTRANCE 1/3

GUERNICA
EXHIBITION

PATRONS

Gerald BARRY, Esq.
Fenner BROCKWAY, Esq.
The Rt. Hon. the Viscount
     CECIL of CHELWOOD, P.C., K.C.
Sir Peter CHALMERS MITCHELL,
     C.B.E., LL.D., F.R.S.
Douglas COOPER, Esq.
Hugh Sykes DAVIES, Esq
Professor Bonamy DOBREE
George EUMORFOPOULOS, Esq., F.S.A.
E. M. FORSTER, Esq.
Victor GOLLANCZ, Esq.
Ashley HAVINDEN, Esq.
A. P. HERBERT, M.P.
Julian S. HUXLEY, Esq. D.Sc., F.R.S
E. McKNIGHT KAUFFER, Esq.
David LOW, Esq.
D. MITRINOVITCH, Esq.
Mrs. Naomi MITCHESON
P. J. NOEL BAKER, M.P.
The Rt. Hon. Lord NOEL-BUXTON, P.C.
Harry POLLITT, Esq.
Miss Eleanor RATHBONE, M.P.
Ruthven TODD, Esq.
Professor TREND
Peter WATSON, Esq.
Mrs. Virginia WOOLF

ORGANISING COMMITTEE

Chairman: Wilfrid ROBERTS, M.P.
Vice-Chairman: Herbert READ, Esq.
The Rt. Hon. the Earl of LISTOWEL
Hon. Treasurer: Roland A. PENROSE, Esq.
Hon. Organiser: E. L. T, MESENS, Esq.
Hon. Secretary: Mrs. Sybil STEPHENSON

OCTOBER 4TH—29TH
DAILY 10 a.m.—5.30 p.m.

IN AID OF THE NATIONAL
JOINT COMMITTEE FOR SPANISH RELIEF

Figure 53
Announcement of
Guernica's exhibition
at the New Burlington
Galleries, London,
4–29 October 1938

1926, and Picasso was an inveterate moviegoer.[18] In Eisenstein's unforgettable montage sequence at the Odessa steps, he repeated key motifs rapidly over and over again so that they remained indelibly in the minds of his audience: the bleeding woman with the baby carriage, the woman carrying the dead child, and the elderly lady with the broken spectacles (figs. 54–56). It is noteworthy that all of these images are of women's reactions to tragedy. Noteworthy too is the similarity between Picasso's juxtaposition of seemingly disparate images in *Guernica* and Eisenstein's jarring intercutting of diverse elements. There is a montage effect in *Guernica* necessitating the consumption of individual motifs and an additive consideration of them. This process requires prolonged, repeated viewing (as does *Potemkin* to fully comprehend its meaning). Both Picasso and Eisenstein—Picasso in his many bust-length painted portraits and Eisenstein in his use of individually indelible motifs— recognized the immense power of a single iconic image to engage and move their audiences.

Picasso sought to be effective in making political statements. During the summer of 1937 he wanted to broadcast the message

June to December 1937

Figure 54
Sergei Eisenstein
Potemkin
1926
Still from the
"Odessa steps" sequence
The Museum of Modern
Art, Film Stills Archive

Figure 55
Sergei Eisenstein
Potemkin
1926
Still from the
"Odessa steps" sequence
The Museum of Modern
Art, Film Stills Archive

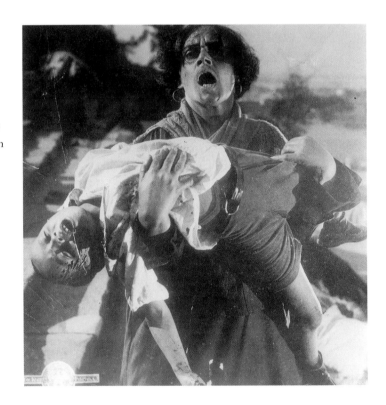

Figure 56
Sergei Eisenstein
Potemkin
1926
Still from the
"Odessa steps" sequence
The Museum of Modern
Art, Film Stills Archive

embodied in *Guernica* as widely as possible. Consequently he did not plunge into any large-scale painting, working instead on prints, which ideally could be disseminated far more readily than even touring paintings. During early July he focused on etching a weeping woman. His very first attempts took place on 1 July, when he began work on a large plate. In the first state (fig. 57) he quickly outlined the figure, based on the general compositional arrangement of the 23 June head (fig. 47). He removed the mantilla but retained the handkerchief. Both hands are visible; the hand with the handkerchief has long, pointed nails while the other appears to have short, broken ones.[19] In the second state (fig. 58) Picasso eliminated one eye and began to rework the top of the head. In the third (fig. 59) Picasso added considerable detail to the woman. He gave her individual strands of hair, restored her left eye, textured her handkerchief, and modeled her face and fingers, evoking the tiniest creases in her skin. Darks and lights were strengthened in the fourth state (fig. 60) and the density of line increased. In the fifth state (fig. 61) Picasso began eliminating elements, clarifying in particular the bridge of the nose and the two eye sockets. Obviously he decided that he had sacrificed too much detail, because in the sixth state (fig. 62) he restored densely etched areas to the hair, neck, cheeks, handkerchief, and eyes.

Figure 57
Weeping Woman
1 July 1937, state 1
Etching, aquatint, and
drypoint on paper
27 ¼ x 19 ½ in.
(69.2 x 49.5 cm)
Musée Picasso, Paris
(MPP 2741)

Figure 58

Weeping Woman
1 July 1937, state II
Etching, aquatint, and
drypoint on paper
27 ¼ x 19 ½ in.
(69.2 x 49.5 cm)
Musée Picasso, Paris
(MPP 2742)

Figure 59

Weeping Woman
1 July 1937, state III
Etching, aquatint, and
drypoint on paper
27 ¼ x 19 ½ in.
(69.2 x 49.5 cm)
Frederick Mulder

Figure 60

Weeping Woman
1 July 1937, state IV
Etching, aquatint, and
drypoint on paper
27 ¼ x 19 ½ in.
(69.2 x 49.5 cm)
Musée Picasso, Paris
(MPP 2745)

Figure 61
Weeping Woman
1 July 1937, state v
Etching, aquatint, and
drypoint on paper
27 ¼ x 19 ½ in.
(69.2 x 49.5 cm)
Musée Picasso, Paris
(MPP 2746)

Figure 62

Weeping Woman

1 July 1937, state VI

Etching, aquatint, and

drypoint on paper

27 ¼ x 19 ½ in.

(69.2 x 49.5 cm)

Musée Picasso, Paris

(MPP 2748)

Figure 63
Weeping Woman
1 July 1937, state VII
Etching, aquatint,
and drypoint on paper
27 ¼ x 19 ½ in.
(69.2 x 49.5 cm)
Musée Picasso, Paris
(MPP 2749

The paths of the tears are dominant. In the final state (fig. 63) Picasso added drypoint in many areas, casting large sections of the face, handkerchief, and hair into richly inked darkness.

Altogether Picasso printed forty proofs of the various states of this head. In only two states did he choose to number his impressions (III and VI, with fifteen each). In the end he did not produce a large edition; why is unclear. Perhaps he was dissatisfied with some aspect of the composition. The density of line certainly seems to have been the most pressing issue, because Picasso redrew the motif again on a smaller scale on 4 July. In the third state of this print (fig. 64) he pushed the hairline back, added more tears, thickened the eyebrows and lashes, and reduced the size of the handkerchief. He returned to the snout-like nose of the 24 May study (fig. 24) but added an architectural frame around her, so that she appears to be set in a particular space rather than floating in some indeterminate zone. His most significant innovation, however, was having the woman bite the handkerchief as she wiped her tears. Picasso redrew the image on another plate (fig. 65); here the reversed head is narrower, the hair more tangled, the features more distorted and disfigured. The walls and ceiling of the room are striped. As before, the woman bites on her handkerchief. Once more Picasso chose not to issue an edition of the print; he retained both plates and printed them in very small quantities in 1949.

Picasso drew two additional weeping women in early July. Traditionally dated to 4 July, the first (fig. 66) is inscribed on its lower right simply "juillet 37." It is probable that this small pen-and-ink drawing is Picasso's reconsideration of the 1 and 4 July etchings. Her face closely resembles the profile in the former, but she bites her handkerchief as in the latter; key changes are the inclusion of the mantilla and the reconfigured fanlike handkerchief. The most extraordinary feature, however, is the density of line. Picasso compressed hundreds of strokes into the face, mantilla, and background of this drawing and by so doing mapped out every nuance of its darks and lights, its dense and open areas. It is as if Picasso resolved whatever problems he had with the head

Figure 64
Weeping Woman
4 July 1937, state III
Drypoint and aquatint
on paper
13 ⅝ x 9 ⅝ in.
(34.5 x 24.6 cm)
Private collection

Figure 65
Weeping Woman
4 July 1937, state IV
Drypoint on paper
13 ⅝ x 9 ⅞ in.
(34.7 x 25 cm)
Private collection

by meticulously tracing every square millimeter of the face and its surroundings with his pen. In a second, even smaller drawing (fig. 67) Picasso drew the same profile as he had in the third-state print of 4 July (fig. 64), but he substantially reworked her forehead and eyes and reconfigured her handkerchief. Her attire is new as well. Picasso's return to paper suggests that he needed to rethink the composition once more.

Also in the first week of July Picasso resumed his stream-of-consciousness writing. He touched on many subjects, but certain phrases recur. The running topos is food and particularly the odors of certain foods: sardines, onions, stale chèvre.[20] Picasso did not celebrate food in these writings; for him it was something rotting, stinking, disintegrating.

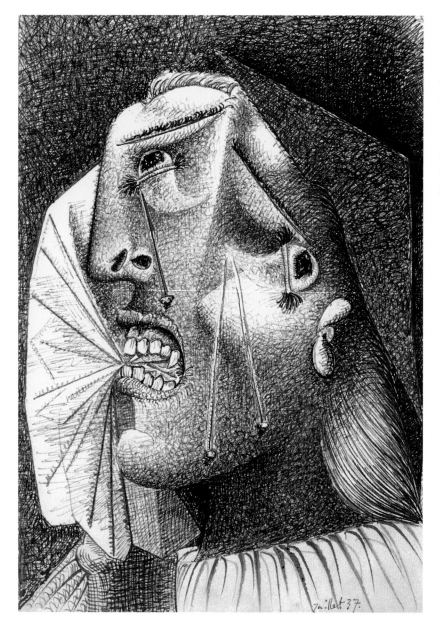

Figure 66
Weeping Woman
with Handkerchief
4 July 1937
Pen and ink on paper
10 x 6 ⅝ in.
(25.5 x 17 cm)
Museo Nacional Centro
de Arte Reina Sofía,
Madrid

Figure 67
*Weeping Woman
with Handkerchief*
6 July 1937
Pen and ink on tan paper
6 x 4 ½ in.
(15.2 x 11.4 cm)
Museo Nacional Centro
de Arte Reina Sofía,
Madrid

His treatment of food in his jottings from 5 through 24 July reveals his feelings about civilization in the age of Franco. Interspersed among his culinary allusions are military and battle references, as in the 6 July entry:

then gunbarrels are organ-mounted tied to piles of cheeses dipping his fingers in the cream of the concrete fact of the flutes and the baying piled on sieves and they burned incense and old rags previously dipped in gasoline and the lieutenant said to his men now that the enemy no longer shows his face press forward the flags we left soaking in brine can wait till reveille hands clasped and feet warm the general sleeps and her daughter does housework [21]

Picasso's writings grew progressively more convoluted; toward the end of the month he wrote, "syncope stretches her long limbs around the neck of the asphodel well displayed in the center of the top ribs smoking her pipe." [22]

By the end of July Picasso was on vacation. For the second summer in a row he and Dora Maar traveled to Mougins, near Cannes in the south of France, where they stayed at the Hôtel Vaste-Horizon. Picasso brought his new dog, an Afghan hound named Kasbec. It was a very social summer: they were joined by Roland Penrose, Paul Eluard and his model-wife, Nusch, the photographer and Dada artist Man Ray and his companion Ady, Christian Zervos, publisher of *Cahiers d'art*, and the photographer Lee Miller. Penrose chronicled Picasso's August and September in Mougins:

Unlike the previous visit, when he had been content to make drawings in a small room with no more than the strict essentials, he installed himself in the only room with a balcony in the hotel. When he emerged on to the terrace for meals he would tell his friends, who were then occupying the entire hotel, what he had been doing. Sometimes he had painted a landscape of the little town...but more often he would announce that he had made a portrait. As a reaction to his recent preoccupation with tragedy, he was seized with a diabolical playfulness." [23]

This playfulness is manifested in garishly colored portraits and land-scapes. Compared with the relatively subdued weeping women he left behind in his Paris studio, the Mougins portraits are painted in rich tones: crimson, pink, azure, mauve, yellow, chartreuse. In several of these Miller was dressed and coiffed as a woman from Arles wearing local garb (fig. 68); so too was Nusch Eluard. Portraits of Nusch (fig. 69) are especially caricatured. They are diametrically opposed in hue and disposition to the weeping figures of May and June 1937 and represent Picasso's liberation from the weighty issues he had been exploring less than one month earlier in Paris.

Despite the differences in the work he produced there, Picasso's routine in Mougins indicates that he was actively scavenging for potential forms and ideas. Penrose reported:

In the morning the beaches provided the main attraction. Sun-bathing with the party of friends from Mougins and frequent dips in the sea would be the prelude to searches along the beach for pebbles, shells, and roots or anything that had been transformed by the action of the waves. The small, neat, well-built physique of Picasso was at home in these surroundings....During one of his wanderings with Dora they found among the rocks, not far from an old refuse dump, the bleached skull of an ox which had been scoured by the sea. With his usual delight in disguises Picasso, closing his eyes, posed for Dora to take his photo-graph, holding in one hand the skull and in the other a staff such as he had put into the hand of the blind Minotaur. [24]

Man Ray's recollections were of relaxed, slow days that were produc-tive nonetheless: "After a morning on the beach and a leisurely lunch, we retired to our respective rooms for a siesta and perhaps love-making. But we worked, too."[25]

Picasso's portrait of Lee Miller was likely one of the last can-vases completed in Mougins, but even before his return to Paris in mid-September he renewed his explorations of the imagery with which he had grappled in early July. He drew a grotesque Ubu Roi figure in one of his notebooks (fig. 70), and he resumed writing. His texts, even when brief, indicate his unabated concern with developments in Spain: "the

Figure 68
Portrait of Lee Miller
as an Arlesienne
20 September 1937
Oil on canvas
31 7/8 x 25 5/8 in.
(81 x 65 cm)
Musée Réattu, Arles,
deposited by the state

Figure 69

Portrait of Nusch Eluard

1937

Oil on canvas

21 ⁵/₈ x 18 ¹/₈ in.

(55 x 46 cm)

The Heinz Berggruen

collection, on loan to

The National Gallery,

London

marquess of christian buttocks throwing a coin at the moorish soldiers
defenders of the virgin."[26]

    It is nearly impossible to confuse most of the post-Mougins
pictures with those Picasso completed before his vacation. The themes
may have remained the same but the motifs used to develop them had
changed. The individual ideograms used to describe each face were
freshly invented; the compositions too were reconsidered and developed
anew. The first of the new group, a relatively large canvas of a mother
with dead child (fig. 71), borrows a mantilla from the 26 June painting
(fig. 47) and the giant hand from other *Guernica* studies (figs. 28 and 31).

Figure 70

At the End of the Jetty

12 September 1937

Pen and ink on paper

11 ¹/₄ x 8 ¹/₄ in.

(28.5 x 21 cm)

John Eastman,

New York

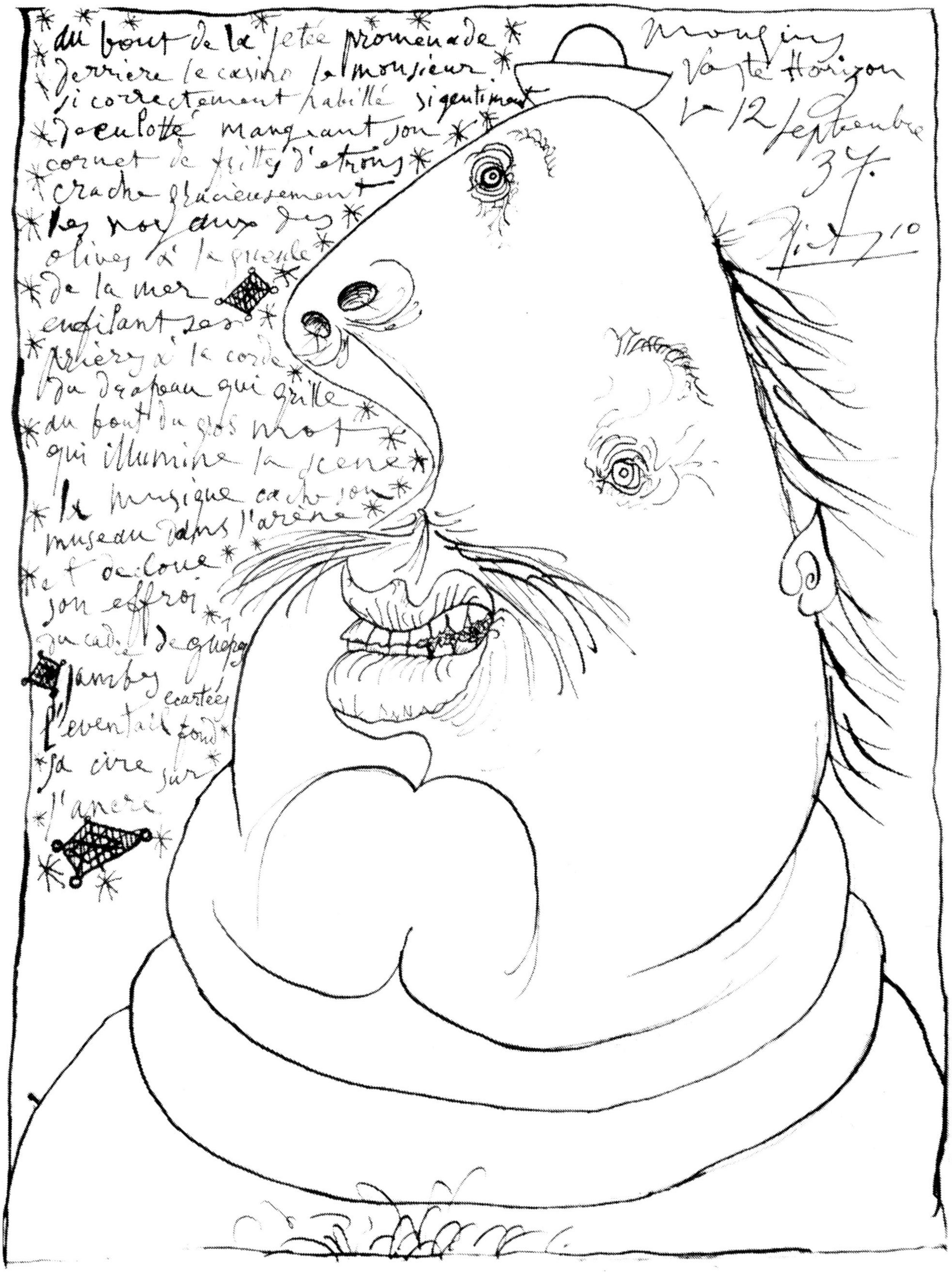
Au bout de la jetée promenade
derrière le casino le monsieur
si correctement habillé si gentiment
déculotté mangeant son
cornet de frites d'étrons
crache gracieusement
les noyaux des
olives à la gueule
de la mer
la musique cache son
museau dans l'arène
son effroi
l'éventail
Mougins
Vaste Horizon
le 12 septembre
37.
Picasso

Figure 71

Mother with Dead Child

26 September 1937

Oil and canvas

51 ⅛ x 76 ¾ in.

(130 x 195 cm)

Museo Nacional Centro

de Arte Reina Sofía,

Madrid

The woman's face is extremely irregular in shape, her body distorted and dramatically foreshortened. The most striking change, however, occurs in the mother's eyes, which have become like small buoys or little boats at sea. Now the tears fall into these boats, vessels able to contain them. These are the signature eyes of the weeping women from the autumn of 1937.

His 12 October drawing (fig. 72) is a reworking of drawings of 8, 13, and 26 June (figs. 36, 38, 40). The shape of the face is essentially the same, and the mouth is a close adaptation, but Picasso significantly altered the teeth, ears, and eyes. The teeth prominently include a sharpened one; the ear is a flower. The eyes are saucers: one holds what appears to be a piece of fruit, the other a candle. Tears pour from them. One day later he used the saucer-eyes again (fig. 73), repositioning them (and redrawing the contours of the face) so that they appear to be sliding

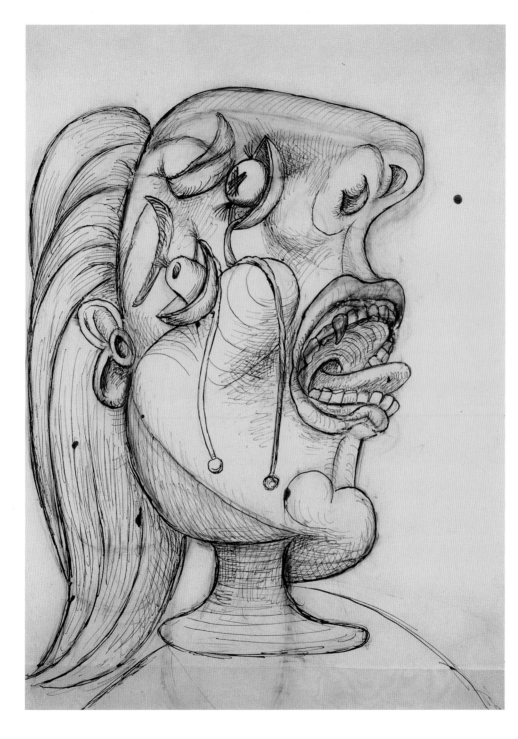

Figure 72
Weeping Woman
12 October 1937
Pen, ink, and pencil
on paper
35 ³⁄₈ x 23 in.
(90 x 58.5 cm)
Museo Nacional Centro
de Arte Reina Sofía,
Madrid

down the woman's cheeks rather than sitting comfortably in their sockets. The ear is a saucer as well. The woman holds a handkerchief to the
far side of her face and is shown with an open mouth, as if she is in the
midst of a scream or a wail.

These two drawings were preparations for three paintings of
the following week. On 17 October Picasso essentially drew the weep-

Figure 73
*Weeping Woman
with Handkerchief*
13 October 1937
Oil and ink on canvas
21 ⁵/₈ x 18 ¹/₈ in.
(55 x 46 cm)
Museo Nacional Centro
de Arte Reina Sofía,
Madrid

ing woman figure on canvas (fig. 74). He tilted the saucer-eyes so that the tears flow down her face in gentle curves. She wears a mantilla and chews on her clutched handkerchief. This version is composed of crisp, unbroken forms with clear lines. The next day Picasso painted the weeping woman image twice. The first seems to have begun its life as a portrait, probably of Dora Maar because of her long, dangling, dark hair

Figure 74
*Weeping Woman
with Handkerchief*
17 October 1937
Oil on canvas
36 ¹/₄ x 28 ³/₄ in.
(92 x 73 cm)
Museo Nacional Centro
de Arte Reina Sofía,
Madrid

(fig 75). Picasso added a handkerchief, drew fishlike eyes (recalling those of his May and June drawings), added a line to represent tears and then scraped away at the paint, leaving thin scratches all over the surface and thick streaks for hair. It is a disquieting painting, with its turbulent surface and its purple and green tones. His second painting of the day is also disturbing because of its tonality and its doubly shrouded eyes (fig. 76). This weeping woman is placed against a dark ground, and her

Figure 75
Weeping Woman
18 October 1937
Oil on canvas
21 ¾ x 18 ¼ in.
(55.3 x 46.3 cm)
Musée Picasso, Paris
(MP 165)

features are colored with greys, purples, and greens. Her eyes are saucers with floating eyeballs. Thick, black strands of hair neatly frame her face, and her tongue is visible through her parted lips. On the one hand she is an image of composure, clasping firmly and assuredly onto her handkerchief. On the other hand her angst-ridden eyes contain barely controllable grief. Picasso kept these two 18 October paintings for himself, neither selling them nor sending them with *Guernica* when it traveled

Figure 76
*Weeping Woman
with Handkerchief*
18 October 1937
Oil on canvas
21 ⁵⁄₈ x 18 ¹⁄₈ in.
(55 x 46 cm)
National Gallery of
Victoria, Melbourne.
Purchased by
The Art Foundation
of Victoria with the
assistance of the Jack and
Genia Liberman family
and donors of The Art
Foundation of Victoria
1984

Figure 78

Weeping Woman
24 October 1937
Oil and ink on paper
10 x 6 ¾ in.
(25.5 x 17.3 cm)
Musée Picasso, Paris
(MP 1192)

abroad. From 12 to 18 October he created only weeping women; and he did not abandon the theme even when several other images—two portraits, two horses— concurrently occupied him during the subsequent week. On 22 October he worked on a print of the subject (fig. 77), again placing the woman (in her Spanish mantilla) in front of a wall, a composition with origins in several *Guernica* studies (figs. 29–30, 41–42, 65). After two states he did not produce a substantial edition. His one significant alteration to the image in this print is the transformation of her tears into two jagged gashes in her cheek, one ending to the side of her mouth, the other pooling around her nostril. He completed a rapidly executed oil study on 24 October (fig. 78). The outline, sketched in strokes of India ink, is generously filled in with patches of color. The handkerchief, held along the side of the face, serves also as a veil. She is seen in half-length for the first time in these compositions. Her face is reduced to simple strokes—a star-furrowed brow, prominently incised cheeks, pebbles for eyes, and a toothless, tongueless mouth.

Figure 77

*Weeping Woman
in Front of a Wall*
22 October 1937, state 1
Aquatint and drypoint
on paper
13 ⁷/₁₆ x 9 ⁵/₈ in.
(34.1 x 24.5 cm)
Los Angeles County
Museum of Art,
Graphic Arts Council
Fund

The repeated and varied inclusion of a handkerchief in these pictures shows Picasso's determination to use the motif effectively. Two small sketches underscore this fact. On 24 October he quickly filled a sheet with tiny heads and hands engulfed by their handkerchiefs (fig 79). In the upper right corner two hands hold a handkerchief that obscures all but two eyes, which appear at the very top edge of the cloth. Two days later he scribbled ideas on the back of an envelope (fig. 80): a

Figure 79
Sheet of Studies:
Weeping Woman
24 October 1937
Pen and ink on paper
10 x 7 in.
(25.5 x 17.9 cm)
Musée Picasso, Paris
(MP 1193)

saucer eye with its cascading tears appears at left; another is at the very top. The rest of the drawing consists of giant handkerchiefs propped up by hidden arms balancing saucer-eyes that spill out to "cry" on the cloth. Instead of resolving these handkerchiefs in relation to appropriately scaled heads, Picasso embues them with a life of their own so that they seem as animated as Miró's ghostlike anthropomorphic apparitions of the same year (fig. 81).

At the end of October Picasso painted two weeping women that he sold relatively soon after he created them. His 28 October ink-and-wash drawing (fig. 82) is a remarkable study that combines elements of the autumn images with the pathos of the June imagery. Picasso's technique of combining scribbled details with crude, almost awkward outlines summarizes the uncontrollable despair of this woman. The figure's ears are knots, her eyes are saucers, her teeth are crooked and jagged, and her nose is snoutlike. Her hair is cloaked in a mantilla, and she gnaws on her handkerchief in anguish, holding it with a clenched hand that is so astutely observed that it captures all of her tension and pain. In this image Picasso used all of the elements with which he had grappled since May and brought them into balance; the result is a succinct but potent statement of grief.

Two days earlier he had painted another image (fig. 83) that contained the same motifs—saucer-eyes, knotted ears, looping tears—yet it was altogether different in effect

Figure 80
Sheet of Studies: Tears
26 October 1937
Pen and ink on the back of an envelope
8 ¹⁄₈ x 6 ½ in.
(20.5 x 16.6 cm)
Musée Picasso, Paris
(MP 1194)

Figure 81
Joan Miró
Untitled
1937
Oil on wood
38 1/8 x 6 5/8 x 7/8 in.
(97 x 16.8 x 2.2 cm)
Musée national d'art
moderne, Centre
Georges Pompidou, Paris

Figure 82
(page 118)
Weeping Head
28 October 1937
Oil wash and ink on
paper
15 5/8 x 10 3/16 in.
(40 x 26.1 cm)
Fogg Art Museum,
Harvard University Art
Museums, Cambridge,
Massachusetts.
Purchase—
Francis H. Burr
Memorial Fund,
1940.155

Figure 83
(page 119)
Weeping Woman
26 October 1937
Oil on canvas
23 1/2 x 19 1/4 in.
(59.7 x 48.9 cm)
Tate Gallery, London

from the 28 October drawing. Its color was strong and assertive. Harsh yellows, reds, purples, and greens dominate the painting. It recalls Picasso's portrait of Marie-Thérèse Walter of seven months earlier (fig. 84) in its saturated color and elaborated setting. Penrose, who lived with this *Weeping Woman* from November 1937 until his death in 1982, accurately captures its power:

In color it is very different from the studies made before going to Mougins. The lurid acid effects had been exchanged for brilliant contrasts—red, blue, green, and yellow. The result of using color in a manner so totally unassociated with grief, for a face in which sorrow is evident in every line, is highly disconcerting. As though the tragedy had arrived with no warning, the red and blue hat is decked with a blue flower. The white handkerchief pressed to her face hides nothing of the agonized grimace on her lips: it serves merely to bleach her cheeks with the color of death. Her fumbling hands knotted with the pain of her emotion join the teardrops that pour from her eyes. Simultaneously they are her fingers, her hand-kerchief and the tears that fall like a curtain of rain heralding the storm. Her eyes like those of Dora Maar are rimmed with black lashes; they nestle in shapes like small boats that have capsized in the tempest, emptying out a river of tears. As the stream follows across the contour of her cheek it passes her ear, the form of which is not unlike a bee come to distill honey from the salt of despair. Finally as we look into the eyes themselves we recognize the reflection of the man-made vulture which has changed her delight into unbearable pain.[27]

The 26 October painting, which Penrose very likely bought from Picasso on 9 November,[28] closed a chapter for Picasso. He was not particularly prolific during November and December of 1937, and he did not repeatedly return to the theme of the weeping woman in the way that he had in previous months. There are, however, isolated exceptions. The first occurred toward the end of November, when he painted a woman chewing on a snaillike handkerchief (fig. 85). Her tar-getlike eyes have floated to the top and side of her head, and her lips are brightly painted. Two large tears fall down her cheek, a return to an earlier and simpler technique of representation, and are silhouetted against it. She is clad in a striped blouse very much like those Picasso wore when

Figure 84
*Woman with Beret
and Collar*
6 March 1937
Oil on canvas
24 x 19 ⁵/₈ in.
(61 x 50 cm)
Private collection

vacationing in the south of France. Her nervous chewing and her tilted-back head are the embodiment of anxiety; she chews at her handkerchief much as she might bite on her fingernails or tear out her hair.

Near the end of the year Picasso chose a small piece of wood for a panel painting of a weeping woman seen from head to toe (fig. 86).[29] She stands before what appears to be a wall broken by a large window with a view of the water. Her hands are raised. Her flesh balloons between each joint of her fingers. Her face is a mask resembling the chiseled features of the weeping heads of the previous May and June (figs. 24–25, 32–34); her body is covered with a black dress atop a lace blouse through which one of her breasts is completely exposed. Her nipple is a bolt, her ear is a nail, her joints are like elastic bands, all mechanical images that convey a sense of palpable torture. She is a kind of primitive yet futuristic monster, a tortured beast suggestive less of immediate grief than of the aftermath of unfathomable horrors.

This painting remained in Picasso's collection until his death. Curiously the Musée Picasso titles it *La suppliante* and translates this as "Crying Woman," yet we see no tears, at least not in the form to which we have become accustomed. Her pose, gesture, and look of total horror are obvious indicators of her grief-stricken state. She is the coda—both chronologically and expressively—to the considerable number of weeping women images Picasso made in 1937. She brings Picasso's tumultuous year to a close. As Gertrude Stein observed:

It was not the events themselves that were happening in Spain which awoke Picasso but the fact that they were happening in Spain, he had lost Spain and here was Spain not lost, she existed, the existence of Spain awakened Picasso, he too existed, everything that had been imposed upon him no longer existed, he and Spain, both of them existed, of course they existed, they exist, they are alive, Picasso commenced to work, he commenced to speak as he has spoken all his life, speaking with drawings and color, speaking with writing, the writing of Picasso.

Figure 85
(page 122)
*Woman with Handkerchief
and Striped Bodice*
20 November 1937
Oil on canvas
21 ¹/₂ x 15 in.
(54.6 x 38.1 cm)
Private collection

Figure 86
(page 123)
Crying Woman
18 December 1937
Gouache and ink
on panel
9 ¹/₂ x 7 ¹/₄ in.
(24 x 18.5 cm)
Musée Picasso, Paris
(MP 168)

All his life he has only spoken like that, he has written like that, and he has been eloquent.

So in 1937 he commenced to be himself again.[30]

Nineteen thirty-seven was the year of Picasso's search for a motif that would articulate the anguish he felt for Spain as well as his own anger. He found it in the weeping women.

Notes

1. Picasso quoted in Simone Téry, "Picasso n'est pas officier dans l'Armée française," *Les Lettres françaises* (24 March 1945); excerpted in Picasso 1972, 149.

2. Penrose 1981B, 88.

3. *"la rabia retorciendo el dibujo de la sombra que lo azota los dientes clavados en la arena y el caballo abierto de par en par al sol que lo lee a las moscas que hilvanan a los nudos de la red llena de boquerones el cohete de azucenas."* Picasso, *Dream and Lie of Franco*, transcribed in Picasso 1989, 166.

4. Christian Zervos, both in *Cahiers d'art* 12, no. 4-5 (1937), 140; and in Zervos 1932–78, vol. 9, no. 53, dates this study to 22 June. The Prado found a note on the back of the drawing dating it 19 June. It is worth noting that Picasso painted two intimate still lifes on 19 June: one of an array of fruit, the other of assorted cakes on a compotier. See Duncan 1961, 223. These paintings remained in Picasso's personal collection until after his death.

5. Picasso gave one of these early identical versions to Dora Maar.

6. Henry Moore quoted by Vera and John Russell in *The Sunday Times* (London) 17 December 1961, 18. Cited by Oppler 1988 202.

7. Penrose, 1981A, 306-7.

8. Sabartès 1949, 5.

9. See the three paintings titled *Woman Crowned with Flowers* reproduced in Duncan 1961, 221 and 225.

10. For excellent discussions of the layout of the pavilion see Freedberg 1986, passim; Chipp, 1988A, 144-51; and Madrid 1987, passim.

11. Eluard, "La Victoire de Guernica," trans. by Roland Penrose in *London Bulletin* 1, no. 6 (October 1938): 7-8.

12. The works of art shown in the pavilion, except for those by artists resident in Paris, were shipped to Valencia at the close of the exhibition, where they disappeared during the chaos of the closing months of the Civil War. In 1986 they were rediscovered and are now on loan from the Spanish government to the Museo de Arte Moderno de Barcelona.

13. Amédée Ozenfant, "Notes d'un touriste à l'exposition," *Cahiers d'art* 12, no. 8-10 (1937): 247; trans. in Oppler 1988, 214-15.

14. The experience of visiting the Spanish pavilion during the summer of 1937 would have been even more powerful than the analogous experience had by visitors to the newly opened United States Holocaust Museum in Washington, D.C., in the spring of 1993. There, both survivors of Nazi Germany and people too young to remember World War II have been horrified by encountering the presentations. Yet these visitors are witnessing a memorial to something that took place half a century before. At the Paris International Exposition viewers confronted documentation of current and ongoing events and the fact that, in Paris, they could do little if anything about the situation.

15. They might also be compared to Peter Paul Rubens' painting *The Horrors of War* (1638). This painting, in the Pitti Palace in Florence, could also be seen as falling within the Spanish patrimony since the Flemish Rubens worked for the Spanish royal family. See Tankard 1984, passim.

16. See Chipp 1988A, 92-4, 105, 127-28.

17. These preparatory studies were not exhibited with the painting in the Spanish pavilion, nor were they shown in Oslo, (at the Kunstnernes Hus), Copenhagen, (at the Statens Museum for Kunst), Stockholm (Liljevalches Konsthall), or Göteborg, Sweden (Konsthallen), where *Guernica* was shown as part of a group exhibition of works by Picasso, Matisse, Georges Braque, and Henri Laurens from January through April 1938.

18. On Picasso's interest in film see Haesserts 1939; Mili 1970; Fernandez Cuenca 1971; Spies, "Picasso—Die Zeit nach Guernica," in Berlin 1992, 17–18; and especially Posada Kubissa 1988.

19. Marie-Thérèse Walter was known for biting her nails; one of Dora Maar's most commented-on features was her tapered fingers with their long red-painted nails. See Gilot and Lake 1964, 14; and Lord 1993, 169.

20. Sabartès noted that Picasso often wrote in the kitchen; Sabartès 1949, 115. Bernadac observed that he must have also written while in the toilet, because several of his poems were on toilet paper; Bernadac, "Painting from the Guts: Food in Picasso's Writings," in Cleveland 1992, 24.

21. *"alors sont montés les canons sur des orgues eux-mêmes attachés à des piles de fromages trempant ses doigts dans la crême du fait concret des flûtes et des abois empilés sur des passoires et on brûla de l'encens et des vieux chiffons qu'on avait trempés auparavant dans la benzine et le lieutenant dit à ses hommes du moment que l'ennemi ne montre pas sa face plus en avant les drapeaux que nous avons mis dans de la saumure peuvent attendre l'heure du réveil les mains jointes et les pieds au chaud la générale dort et sa fille fait le ménage..."* Text of 6 July 1937, Picasso 1989, 172–73.

22. *"la syncope étirait ses longujes pattes autour du cou de l'asphodèle mise bien en évidence au milieu du plat de côte fumant sa pipe."* Text of July 1937. Ibid., 176.

23. Penrose 1981A, 311.

24. Ibid., 312.

25. Man Ray, *Self-Portrait* (New York: McGraw-Hill Book Company, 1963): 227. Apparently Man Ray made his last film during the summer of 1937; it was in color and starred Picasso and Eluard. Neil Baldwin, *Man Ray: American Artist* (New York: Clarkson N. Potter, 1988): 209.

26. *"retrato de la marquesa de culo cristiano echándoles un duro a los soldados moros defensores de la virgen."* The *soldados moros* were a Moroccan troop serving in the Franco-nationalist ranks during the Spanish Civil War. Text of September 1937, Picasso 1989, 176.

27. Penrose 1981A, 314–35.

28. This is based on Penrose's appointment diary of 1937 (Penrose archives, Chiddingly, England). I am grateful to Michael Sweeney, the curator of the Roland Penrose collection, for thoroughly searching these diaries and sending me copies of the relevant pages.

29. There are two other weeping women dated to 1937. One is a *Weeping Head,* charcoal on paper, 11 $\frac{1}{2}$ x 8 $\frac{3}{8}$ in. (29.3 x 21.2 cm) (ex-collection Siegfried Rosengart, Lucerne) (Zervos IX.75); and *Head of a Woman at the Window,* colored crayon on paper, 11 $\frac{3}{8}$ x 9 $\frac{1}{4}$ in. (29 x 23.5 cm) (private collection) (Picasso estate negative number 106029).

30. Gertrude Stein, *Picasso* (Paris: Librairie Floury, 1938); repr. in Stein 1970, 84.

"...the

Muses are women.

"*Woman being the very substance of man's poetic work, it is understandable that she should appear as his inspiration: the Muses are women. A Muse mediates between the creator and the natural springs whence he must draw. Woman's spirit is profoundly sunk in nature, and it is through her that man will sound the depths of silence and of the fecund night. A Muse creates nothing by herself; she is a calm, wise Sibyl, putting herself with docility at the service of a master.*"

—Simone de Beauvoir[1]

"*They're all Picassos, not one is Dora Maar....Do you think I care? Does Madame Cézanne care? Does Saskia Rembrandt care?*"

—Dora Maar, reflecting on Picasso's portraits of her[2]

*P*icasso painted women throughout his career. One can argue that the weeping women are distant cousins of the melancholy ladies of the blue period, the somber nudes of the rose period, the dissected nudes of the cubist years, the neoclassical mannequins of the 1920s, or the protoplasmic masses of the late 1920s and early 1930s.

Certainly not all of the women Picasso depicted are grief-stricken or traumatized; indeed many of them are joyous and seemingly carefree. Nevertheless there are ties between certain key segments of Picasso's oeuvre, particularly beginning in the late 1920s, and the motif of the weeping woman; these ties can tell us something about how he derived the concept from within his already established personal vocabulary. Why a weeping *woman* and not a man, a horse, a bull, a minotaur, a skull, or a bowl of fruit? What attributes of women made them suitable for the emotional messages Picasso sought to convey? Why did the weeping women appear in the same format that he used for portrait heads? The weeping women resonate with social and political messages, yet they function equally as bust-length heads, albeit emotional ones. Picasso's ideogrammatic elements, dominant in the depictions of the weeping women, recur in works seemingly unrelated in theme, and nearly always appear in portraits of women known to him.

We do not need to rewind to Picasso's infancy in order to reconstruct his attitudes toward women. To understand the origins of the weeping women of 1937 we must turn to the late 1920s, the period when his longest stable relationship had begun to sour. We may do so without resorting to the tendency of so many pseudopsychoanalytic Picasso studies to overinterpret the meaning of Picasso's imagery.[3] In this chapter we backtrack to examine Picasso's representations of the three women whose lives were intertwined with his when the weeping women were conceived and developed: Olga Koklova, Marie-Thérèse Walter, and Dora Maar. A straightforward consideration of the relationship between his depictions of them and his life with them helps explain the metamorphosis of these actual women into the potent image of the weeping woman.

Page 128: detail
Woman with a Flower
(Figure 117)

CHAPTER **IV**

Figure 87
Olga Koklova and
Picasso in Rome
March or April 1917

In 1917, when Picasso as set
and costume designer was collab-
orating with impresario Serge
Diaghilev, writer Jean Cocteau,
and composer Erik Satie on
Parade for the Ballets Russes, he
met a twenty-five-year-old
dancer from the troupe (fig. 87).
Olga Koklova was the daughter
of a czarist general. Enamored of her, Picasso followed the company
from Rome to Paris to Madrid to Barcelona amid the continuing turmoil of the First World War. He and Koklova were married in July 1918
and moved shortly thereafter into a two-story apartment on the affluent
rue La Boëtie in the eighth arrondissement of Paris.

Picasso began painting portraits of Koklova even before their
marriage. While she was in Barcelona and still a dancer with Diaghilev's
company, he portrayed her as a Spanish woman with mantilla and shawl

(fig. 88). Later she became classical in appearance, an Ingresque
portrait. He first photographed
her, then painted her (fig. 89), as
the 1917 equivalent of Ingres'
Madame Rivière. In the early
1920s he depicted her as the
essence of maternity (fig. 90)
when she became the mother of
his first child, Paulo.

Most of Picasso's biographers
portray Koklova as a haughty,
snobbish social climber, eager to
be accepted within Parisian aristocratic circles.[4] They suggest
that she was keen to marry
Picasso but are generally silent on

Figure 88
Olga Koklova in a Mantilla
summer–autumn 1917
Oil on canvas
25 ¼ x 20 ⅞ in.
(64 x 53 cm)
Picasso estate

1927-1936

Figure 89
Olga Koklova in
an Armchair
winter 1917
Oil on canvas
51 ¹/₈ x 34 ⁵/₈ in.
(130 x 88 cm)
Musée Picasso, Paris
(MP 55)

Figure 90

Mother and Child

summer 1922

Oil on canvas

38 ³⁄₈ x 32 in.

(97.5 x 81.3 cm)

The Baltimore Museum

of Art, The Cone

Collection, formed by

Dr. Claribel Cone and

Miss Etta Cone of

Baltimore, Maryland

his motivations. Curiously, in the early stages of his courtship of Koklova he met and was immediately attracted to Eugenia Errazuriz, a wealthy Chilean woman prominent in European aristocratic circles (fig. 91). Picasso's friend the art historian Douglas Cooper, who knew Errazuriz, later observed:

He was handsome, but from Eugenia's point of view, his clothes left something to be desired; particularly, to meet the King of Spain, who had asked Diaghilev to present this creation of one of his subjects. Eugenia immediately took Picasso in hand and displayed a serious attachment to this young genius, whom she obliged to undertake a vestimentary transformation of his person, and later, to accompany her to the salons of the beau monde which constituted her circle of friends.[5]

Why he decided to marry Koklova rather than to pursue more aggressively Errazuriz or another woman in wealthy society, if such was his motive, remains one of the great mysteries of his biography. Few of Picasso's biographers to date explain in detail the specific attractions he felt and the relationships he actually consummated.[6] For example, we know that earlier he was devastated by the protracted illness and December 1915 death of his mistress Eva Gouel (Marcelle Humbert); he wrote to Gertrude Stein, "My poor Eva is dead....This has been a great sorrow for me, and I know that you will miss her. She was always so good for me."[7] But at the same time he conducted a clandestine, passionate affair with the youthful Gabrielle Lespinasse, allegedly asking her to marry him only two months later (in February 1916).[8] By October 1916 he could no longer bear to live in the apartment in which Eva had died; he moved to the Paris suburb of Montrouge. In early 1917, when

Figure 91

Picasso with Eugenia Errazuriz (left) and Olga Picasso (right) at a ball given by Comte Etienne de Beaumont for the premiere of the ballet *Mercury,* 1924

Photographed by Man Ray

he was in Rome in the throes of working on *Parade*, he and Cocteau frequently discussed sex and women; once the two compared notes by drawing their penises in their notebooks (**figs. 92–93**). When he met Koklova Picasso was an eligible single man with considerable sexual vitality and was naturally attracted to the worldly social circles surrounding the Ballets Russes. Penrose described their deepening involvement: "The attachment between the Russian ballerina and her Spanish lover had grown rapidly. She spoke French fluently and enjoyed the long fantastic stories that he told her in his thick Spanish accent."[9]

Much later, in her memoirs of her years with the artist,

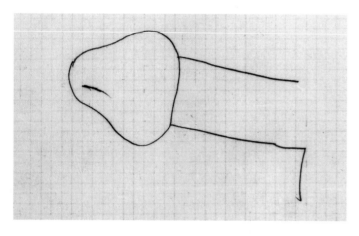

Figure 92
Jean Cocteau
Study
1917
Pencil on paper
Fonds Boris Kochno,
Bibliothèque de l'Opéra,
Paris

Françoise Gilot recounted Picasso's description of the marriage. To be sure, Gilot's account is colored by hostility toward her former lover, but it does contain his attempt to explain his pursuit of Koklova:

He had already told me the story of their difficult life together. He had married her in 1918, when she was a dancer with the Ballets Russes of Diaghilev. She wasn't one of the better dancers in the troupe, he said, but she was pretty and she had another asset that he had found very appealing: she came from a family that belonged to the lower echelons of Russian nobility. Diaghilev, Pablo said, had an original way of choosing his dancers: half of them had to be very good dancers; the other half, pretty girls of good social background....

With Diaghilev he was introduced to another world. Even though basically he disliked that kind of social nonsense, it tempted him for a time and his marriage with Olga corresponded, in a sense, to that momentary temptation.

I could see from the way he spoke of their beginnings that Pablo had thought this well-born young woman would make a very effective partner in a social stratum a good deal higher than the one he had occupied until then....

93a

Figures 93a , b
Studies
1917
Pencil on paper
4 ¾ x 6 ⅞ in. (each)
(12 x 17.5 cm)
Musée Picasso, Paris
(MP 1867)

According to Pablo…she married thinking she was going to lead a soft, pampered, upper-crust life. Pablo figured he would continue to lead the life of a bohème—on a loftier, grander scale, to be sure, but still remain independent.[10]

Despite his denigration of Koklova as someone in search of a "soft, pampered, upper-crust life," that was precisely what Picasso also sought, both while living with her in Montrouge and afterwards. They honey-

93b

mooned at Errazuriz's elegant villa in Biarritz. They spent May 1919 at the Savoy in London while Picasso created sets and costumes for Diaghilev's ballet *The Three-Cornered Hat*, the summer of 1919 at Saint-Raphaël (his first visit to the Côte d'Azur), the summer of 1920 at Juan-les-Pins, the summers

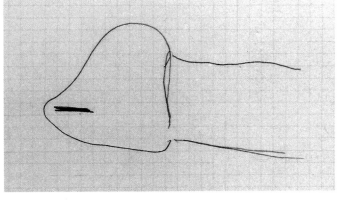

of 1922 and part of 1923 in Dinard (in Brittany), and the remainder of 1923 in Antibes. Picasso's itinerary demonstrates that he was in the thick of French aristocratic circles, flocking to seashore resorts during the annual exodus from Paris in July and August.

During the summer of 1924 Picasso was once again in Antibes with Koklova and Paulo. It was his period of what Gilot described as *"le high-life"*: "with nurse, chambermaid, cook, chauffeur, and all the rest."[11] In addition to the many landscapes he made during this trip he filled several notebooks with mysterious webs of lines whose intersections feature prominent dots.[12] Less than a year later these drawings were reproduced and celebrated in the second number of Breton and Eluard's vanguard journal, *La Révolution surréaliste*; this signaled a shift in Picasso's work away from his heretofore dominant neoclassicism.

Dora Maar observed of Picasso that "when the woman in the artist's life changed, virtually everything else changed."[13] In the case of the 1924 surrealist web drawings the woman had not yet changed, but the shift in style anticipated such a course of events. Picasso's monumental 1925 painting, *The Three Dancers* (fig. 94), contains radically distorted figures. It is his first postwar painting to make use of ideograms to detail a face, hands, and feet. The face of the figure on the left seems to be disintegrating; it is tempting to read the abstract form unfurling from it as a large tear and the figure as an early crying woman.[14]

The surrealists believed in painting as a sign language, with obscure forms and difficult-to-decipher motifs combining to create images;[15] to them Miró, powerfully influenced by neolithic art, was an exemplary painter in this regard. Beginning around 1923 Miró began to use ideograms to represent human features; by 1924 his work was at the center of the surrealist canon.

Picasso in effect announced his own use of ideograms in *The Three Dancers*,[16] one of his most massive paintings since *Les Demoiselles d'Avignon* (1907). Less than two months later the complexity of this usage increased exponentially. In *The Embrace* (fig. 95) two lovers are metamorphosed into two interlocked monsters, their faces like composite masks with stylized features. The embracers are stand-ins for Picasso and Koklova; whatever tenderness they once shared has given way to a vicious devouring of one another. It is a passion engulfed in violence.

Penrose recorded that Picasso "was becoming daily more deeply dissatisfied with the life of a successful and fashionable painter into which he had been enticed by his wife. Her possessiveness was the cause of growing antagonism."[17] Gilot recalled Picasso relating that his wife had torn up letters to him from Apollinaire and Max Jacob.[18] By 1927 Picasso was depicting women—most of whom appear to be Koklova in

Figure 94
The Three Dancers
June 1925
Oil on canvas
84 5/8 x 55 7/8 in.
(215 x 142 cm)
Tate Gallery, London

Figure 95
The Embrace
summer 1925
Oil on canvas
51 ¹/₈ x 38 ¹/₈ in.
(130 x 97 cm)
Musée Picasso, Paris
(MP 85)

disguise—exclusively through ideograms. Much later Picasso spoke of his desire to communicate through a kind of ideogrammatic concision:

I want to say a nude. I don't want to make a nude like a nude. I only want to say breast, say foot, say hand, belly. If I can find the way to say it, that's enough. I don't want to paint the nude from head to foot, but just to be able to say it. That's what I want. When we're talking about it, a single word is enough. Here, one single look and the nude tells you what it is, without a word.[19]

The bust-length portraits of women Picasso created from 1927 through 1929 (as opposed to the contemporaneous bathers) consist chiefly of protoplasmic biting heads. There is little doubt that these symbolize Koklova. The mouth, source of the screaming so vexing to Picasso, is dominant. In two examples (figs. 96–97) the teeth are tendrillike hairs in a huge devouring cavity. Another head has jaws that appear as ser-

Figure 96
Head of a Woman
1927
Oil on canvas
21 ³/₄ x 13 ¹/₄ in.
(55.3 x 33.7 cm)
The Jacques and Natasha
Gelman Collection

Figure 97
Head on a Red Background
1928
Charcoal and oil
on canvas
25 ¹/₂ x 18 ¹/₈ in.
(64.8 x 46 cm)
Quintana Fine Art,
New York

Figure 98
Face
12 February 1929
Crayon, charcoal and oil
on canvas
25 ⅝ x 21 ¼ in.
(65 x 54 cm)
Private collection

rated wedges (fig. 98). In two more (figs. 99–100) the face becomes a large menacing mouth, a skull-like grin that cleaves the eyes apart. Picasso returned repeatedly to the mouth as the focus of these compositions, which are far from the classically inspired portraits of Koklova from the early 1920s; they are more animal than human in inspiration. When a man and a woman appear together in paintings of this period, the encounter is sinister. This was true of *The Embrace* and also of the images from Picasso's "cabana" series of bathers that began in 1927. In *Bust of a Woman with Self-Portrait* (fig. 101), the face is nearly all mouth; the wide-open jaws splitting it down the middle are set to devour the portrait; a threatening *vagina dentata* has been observed by scholars.[20] The nostrils appear at the very top of the head, the eyes are widely separated, and the hair is shown as two large wedges. This is certainly Koklova;[21] she appears before a framed self-portrait of Picasso, a rela-

Figure 99
Woman in a Red Armchair
1929
Oil on canvas
25 ⅝ x 21 ¼ in.
(65 x 54 cm)
The Menil Collection,
Houston

Figure 100
Seated Woman
1927
Oil on canvas
59 x 43 ¼ in.
(150 x 110 cm)
Private collection,
England

tively faithful silhouette in shadow. The two faces, aimed in the same direction, do not engage one another. By 1931 Picasso and Koklova are locked in combat. Picasso's *The Kiss* (fig. 102) is a depiction of two heads devouring each other. It is a much starker image than *The Embrace*, of six years earlier. It was created at a time when Picasso was estranged from Koklova and their relationship had taken a vitriolic turn, as they quarreled over assets including homes, art, and income.

  Picasso, however, had already found a new lover. In January 1927 he approached Marie-Thérèse Walter in front of the Galeries Lafayette department store.[22] Walter later related: "I was seventeen years old. I was an innocent young girl. I knew nothing—either of life or of Picasso....I had gone to do some shopping at the Galeries Lafayette, and

Figure 101
*Bust of a Woman
with Self-Portrait*
February 1929
Oil on canvas
28 x 23 ⅞ in.
(71 x 60.5 cm)
Private collection

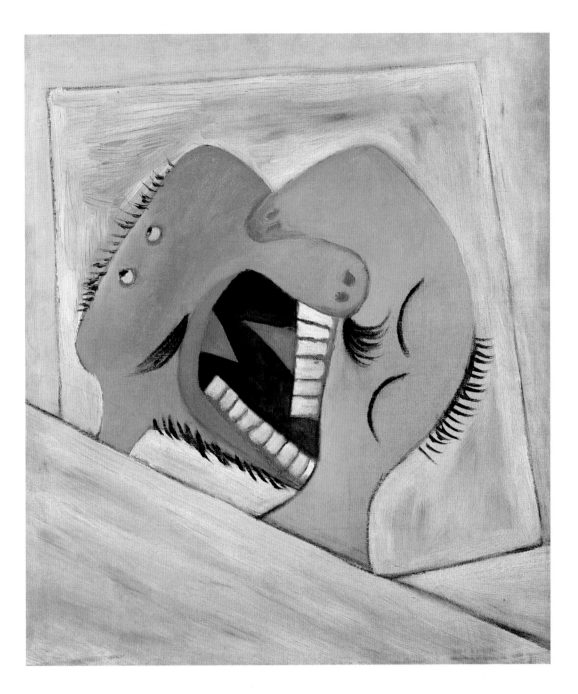

Figure 102

The Kiss

12 January 1931

Oil on canvas

24 x 19 ⅞ in.

(61 x 50.5 cm)

Musée Picasso, Paris

(MP 132)

Picasso saw me leaving the Metro. He simply took me by the arm and said, 'I am Picasso! You and I are going to do great things together.'"[23] Within a week they were lovers, as Walter disclosed to Lydia Gasman in 1972. Picasso kept her existence essentially secret well into the 1960s; during their early relationship he placed coded references to her in pictures by intertwining her initials with his own (fig. 103).[24] Theirs was a

Figure 103

Guitar Hanging on a Wall
1927
Oil on canvas
10 ⁹/₁₆ x 13 ⁵/₈ in.
(26.8 x 34.6 cm)
James W. and Marilynn
Alsdorf Collection,
Chicago

very passionate and clandestine affair from the start. As Walter (figs.
104–5) was underage, Picasso had to be especially discreet. When she
accompanied him to Dinard during the summer of 1928, Picasso
installed her in a pension for children, while he was situated nearby with
his wife and son.[25] By placing her there, he protected himself to a
degree; nevertheless, according to Walter, in Dinard he initiated her
into his preferred sadomasochistic sexual practices.[26]

All of Picasso's visual references to Walter in the later 1920s are
veiled. His depictions of bathers, done in Cannes during a summer away
from Walter in 1927 and continued in Dinard during the following two
summers, consist of sexually suggestive, erectile human tissue, engorged
and twisted into abstract shapes and embellished with facial attributes.[27]
His ball-playing bathers on the beach at Dinard, painted during the
summers of 1928 and 1929, no doubt were inspired by children staying
at Walter's pension. By 1930 Picasso could no longer remain so secretive
about his imagery. He desperately wanted to sculpt; indeed he had
hoped that his bathers would eventually be made into giant statues that
would decorate the promenade at Cannes.[28] In June 1930 he purchased

Figure 104
Marie-Thérèse Walter
c. 1926

Figure 105
Marie-Thérèse Walter
c. 1927

an immense studio at Boisgeloup in Normandy, approximately forty miles from Paris. There, housed within a huge eighteenth-century estate, Picasso sculpted massive heads out of plaster; later they were cast in cement and in bronze (fig. 106). The large bulbous features of these heads were exaggerations of Walter's visage; Picasso modeled them over

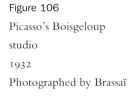

Figure 106
Picasso's Boisgeloup
studio
1932
Photographed by Brassaï

and over until he had developed a distinctive form for a face (fig. 107), consisting of a nose that began at the top of the forehead, bulging eye sockets, and swollen lips. This sculpturally derived profile was employed by Picasso for virtually all of the portraits he produced during the next four decades.

In 1932 Picasso created a body of works depicting Walter asleep (figs. 108–9). These are direct descendents of his Boisgeloup heads. Most often the figure is a fleshy, Titianesque nude posed to underscore her soft, curvilinear shape. John Berger interprets this form from a particularly male perspective that is useful in comprehending Picasso's own thoughts:

What makes these paintings different is the degree of their direct sexuality. They refer without any ambiguity at all to the experience of making love to this woman. They describe sensations and, above all, the sensation of sexual comfort. Even when she is dressed or with her daughter…she is seen in the same way: soft as a cloud, easy, full of precise pleasures, and inexhaustible because alive and sentient. In literature the thrall which a particular woman's body can have over a man has been described often. But words are abstract and can hide as much as they state. A visual image can reveal far more naturally the sweet mechanism of sex. One need only think of a drawing of a breast and then compare it to all the stray associations of the word, to see how this is so. At its most fundamental there aren't any words for sex—only noises; yet there are shapes.[29]

This direct sexuality is suggested by the three simple intersecting lines defining Walter's crotch and vulva in *Nude on a Black Couch* (fig. 108). Healthy, full-grown philodendron leaves appear to sprout from the body of this nude, reinforcing her fecundity. The sexual element is particular-

Figure 107
Head of a Woman
1931
Bronze
30 ¾ x 17 ½ x 21 ¼ in.
(78 x 44.5 x 54 cm)
Musée Picasso, Paris
(MP 298)

Figure 108
(page 148)
Nude on a Black Couch
9 March 1932
Oil on canvas
63 ¾ x 51 ¾ in.
(161.9 x 131.4 cm)
Private collection

Figure 109
(page 149)
The Mirror
12 March 1932
Oil on canvas
51 ½ x 38 ⅛ in.
(130.8 x 96.8 cm)
Private collection

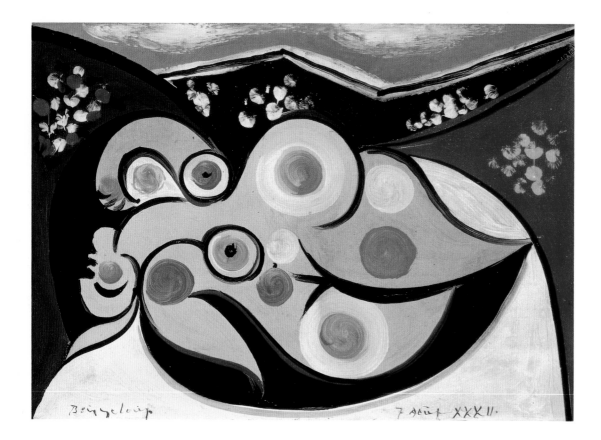

Figure 110
Reclining Woman
7 August 1932
Oil on canvas
9 ½ x 13 in.
(24.1 x 33 cm)
Private collection

ly apparent in *The Mirror* (fig. 109), in which the voluptuous Walter is recumbent before a reflection of her buttocks.

The sleeping Walter is the polar opposite of the 1927–29 *vagina dentata* heads of Koklova (figs. 96–99). She is soft, an organic mass of flesh (figs. 110–12); Koklova is hard-edged. She is compliant, nonthreatening, comfortable; Koklova is hostile, menacing, brutal. Both are depicted as filling their spaces; Picasso framed each figure so that it would be dominant. Walter is painted with vivid hues, particularly violets and greens; Koklova, in contrast, is described through muted rose, browns, blacks, and whites.[30] Each figure represents an emotional extreme. These opposed states were of particular importance to Picasso because they, like the weeping woman motif, served as summary ideograms or metaphors.

It should not be supposed that Picasso dispensed with these menacing images of women in 1929 and never returned to them. Two pictures, both produced during the week of 7 July 1934, indicate that he still retained the notion of woman as threatening beast. In one (fig. 113)

Figure 111
Sleeping Woman
(Marie-Thérèse Walter)
1932
Oil on canvas
10 ⁵⁄₈ x 18 ¹⁄₄ in.
(27 x 46.4 cm)
Private collection

Figure 112
Sleep
1932
Oil on canvas
18 ¹⁄₄ x 18 ¹⁄₄ in.
(46.5 x 46.5 cm)
Private collection

Figure 113

The Murder

10 July 1934

Ink on paper

13 ⅜ x 20 ⅛ in.

(34 x 51 cm)

Musée Picasso, Paris

(MP 1134)

a woman with rubbery arms thrusts a knife into the breast of a sculptural bust of a female. The bust, clearly inspired by Walter, is a descendant of the Boisgeloup heads. The knife-wielding woman, dominated by a huge head with a wide-open mouth and prominent biting teeth, is Picasso's view of Koklova in the early 1930s.

Just one week later Picasso resumed making bust-length, strongly colored portraits of Walter (fig. 114). Rounded edges are supplemented by angular ones; here the organic meets the cubist. When Picasso depicted himself at work at this time (fig. 115), cubist elements

Figure 114

Head

17 July 1934

Oil on canvas

28 ¾ x 23 ⅝ in.

(73 x 60 cm)

Hirshhorn Museum and Sculpture Garden, Washington, D.C., The Joseph H. Hirshhorn Bequest, 1981

encase the serpentine Walter, who languidly reclines before him as he
paints not a nude but a landscape.

In the early 1930s Picasso painted Walter chiefly in two poses:
as a sleeping nude and as a seated woman. In *The Red Armchair* (fig. 116)
the figure is nestled comfortably within the confines of her curving
chair. Her face is doubled: she is shown in profile, yet her features are
also arranged frontally. Her breasts, doubled also, are seen simultaneously

Figure 115
The Studio
1934
Oil on canvas
50 ³/₈ x 62 ³/₄ in.
(128 x 159.3 cm)
Indiana University Art
Museum, Bloomington,
Indiana, Gift of Dr. and
Mrs. Henry R. Hope
69.55

Figure 116
The Red Armchair
16 December 1931
Oil and enamel on ply-
wood
51 ¹/₂ x 39 in.
(130.8 x 99 cm)
Art Institute of Chicago,
Gift of Mr. and Mrs.
Daniel Saidenberg

from the front and from below. The dual nature of the portrait once
again raises the issue of Picasso's view of the separate aspects of Walter's
character: her personality and her sensuality.

His *Woman with a Flower* (fig. 117) is a paean to her sensual side.
Walter is seated in an armchair, but she is far less contained by it than
before. She is partly humanoid, partly vegetal; her breasts are like fruits,

Figure 117
Woman with a Flower
10 April 1932
Oil on canvas
63 ¾ x 51 ⅛ in.
(162 x 130 cm)
Private collection

Figure 118
Henri Matisse
The Yellow Robe
1929–31
Oil on canvas
39 ¼ x 31 ¾ in.
(99.7 x 80.6 cm)
The Baltimore Museum
of Art, The Cone
Collection, formed by Dr
Claribel Cone and Miss
Etta Cone of Baltimore,
Maryland

her arms like leaves. Her face is a composite ideogram, with a circle of teeth around an empty mouth cavity; two tiny eyes float within a kidney-shaped, animallike face, and a bulging nose protrudes between them. Both her face and her body are erogenous, gaping organic orifices that invite exploration.

"When I paint a woman in an armchair," Picasso observed, "the armchair implies old age or death...or else the armchair is there to protect her."[31] He painted women in armchairs during his blue period, during his cubist years, and during his neoclassical phase. In the 1930s these chair-bound women directly responded to Matisse's work as well. Matisse painted many of his models in lavishly decorated interiors, often seating them on elaborately upholstered chairs or on divans. A comparison of a Matisse (fig. 118) with a Picasso in this format discloses dramatic differences. Matisse's model is placed in open, palpable space, in contrast with the compression in Picasso's *Red Armchair*. She is emotionally removed as well, whereas we sense that Picasso knew his model intimately from the way he painted her rounded forms and emphasized her intense gaze, capturing her salient features. She engages us as she engaged the artist. Matisse's model looks into space with indistinct pupils; those of Picasso's figure are prominent and focused.

When Picasso was painting these portraits of the sleeping and seated Marie-Thérèse Walter, their relationship was in a relatively contented phase. Koklova allegedly discovered their involvement when she saw her husband's June 1932 retrospective at Galerie Georges Petit in Paris.[32] By this time Picasso's affair with Walter had intensified. He spent the summer of 1932 in Boisgeloup with her while Koklova and their son Paulo were in Juan-les-Pins. During the following summer Walter remained in Paris for a portion of the season and then traveled to Biarritz; Picasso, Koklova, and Paulo vacationed in Cannes and Barcelona. While in Spain Picasso wrote to Walter daily.[33] She was reasonably happy; although his lovemaking was "at times intimidating and 'terrible,'" as Gasman reported her saying, it "was also in the end a completely fulfilling experience. Picasso, she could not forget, was very 'virile.'" Walter recounted that "il me couvrait de son amour" (he covered me with his love).[34] The erotic etchings produced by Picasso at this time for the *Vollard Suite* testify to his passion for Walter, the sensual partner, as well as to his contempt for Koklova, the menacing, monstrous woman.

The relative equilibrium Picasso had reached was upset early in 1935. Life at home was already somewhat turbulent; in the fall of 1933 his first long-term companion, Fernande Olivier, published her memoirs. Picasso unsuccessfully tried to suppress the book. The already outraged Koklova's fury was boundless when she learned in the spring of 1935 that Walter was pregnant. With Paulo she moved into the Hotel California in Paris. Walter gave birth to a daughter, Maya, on 5 October. On the birth certificate the father was listed as unknown, but Picasso was named as godfather.

Picasso contemplated divorcing Koklova, but she adamantly refused to consider it and, as retribution, placed seals on his property, including much of his work and even his paints and brushes.[35] Picasso recognized that he could not divorce her without losing a large proportion of his assets; the application of community property laws in his case would have crippled his career. By the end of 1935 they had resolved certain issues: Koklova assumed full custody of Paulo and received Boisgeloup.

Picasso was devastated. He later told the photographer David Douglas Duncan that it was "the worst time of my life."[36] He essentially stopped working as a visual artist and began writing for several months.

His friend and collector Gertrude Stein described this phase:

So Picasso ceased to work.

It was very curious.

He commenced to write poems but this writing was never his writing. After all the egoism of a painter is not at all the egoism of a writer, there is nothing to say about it, it is not. No.

Two years of not working. In a way Picasso liked it, it was one responsibility the less, it is nice not having responsibilities, it is like the soldiers during a war, a war is terrible, they said, but during a war one has no responsibility, neither for death, nor for life. So these two years were like that for Picasso, he did not work, it was not for him to decide every moment what he saw, no, poetry for him was something to be made during rather bitter meditations, but agreeably enough, in a café.

This was his life for two years, of course he who could write, write so well with drawings and with colors, knew very well that to write with words was, for him, not to write at all. Of course he understood that but he did not wish to allow himself to be awakened, there are moments in life when one is neither dead nor alive and for two years Picasso was neither dead nor alive, it was not an agreeable period for him, but a period of rest, he, who all his life needed to empty himself and to empty himself, during two years he did not empty himself, that is to say not actively, actually he really emptied himself completely, emptied himself of many things and above all of being subjugated by a vision which was not his own vision."[37]

Picasso wrote voluminously in 1935 and 1936. While he did in fact continue to produce art, it was to an extremely limited degree. His stream-of-consciousness writings, in the rhythmic nature of their repetitions and cadences and their violent imagery, are entirely in sync with his anger at Koklova at the time. He refers to her in several of his 1935 texts as an "evil tongue" or a "tongue of fire."[38]

The graphic conjurings found in his writings have numerous ties to a series of very elaborate ideogrammatic images he created two years earlier (fig. 119). In these studies Picasso expanded the motifs begun in the *vagina dentata* heads of the late 1920s. Here the female form

Figure 119
(Pages 160–64)
An Anatomy
Published in *Minotaure*,
no. 1 (1933)

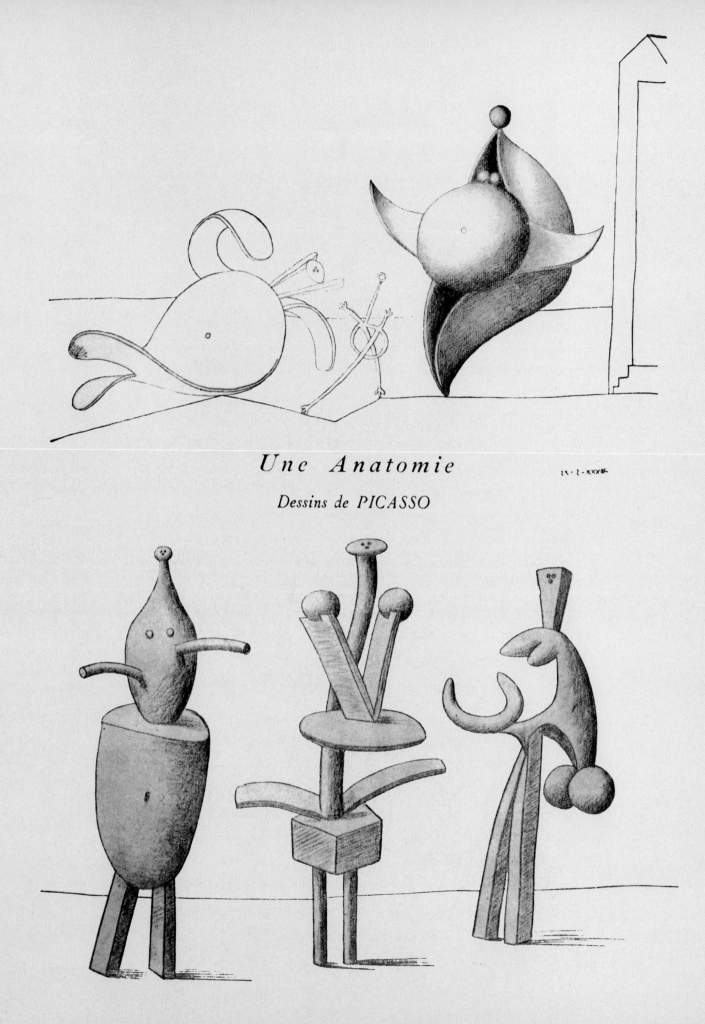

Une Anatomie

Dessins de PICASSO

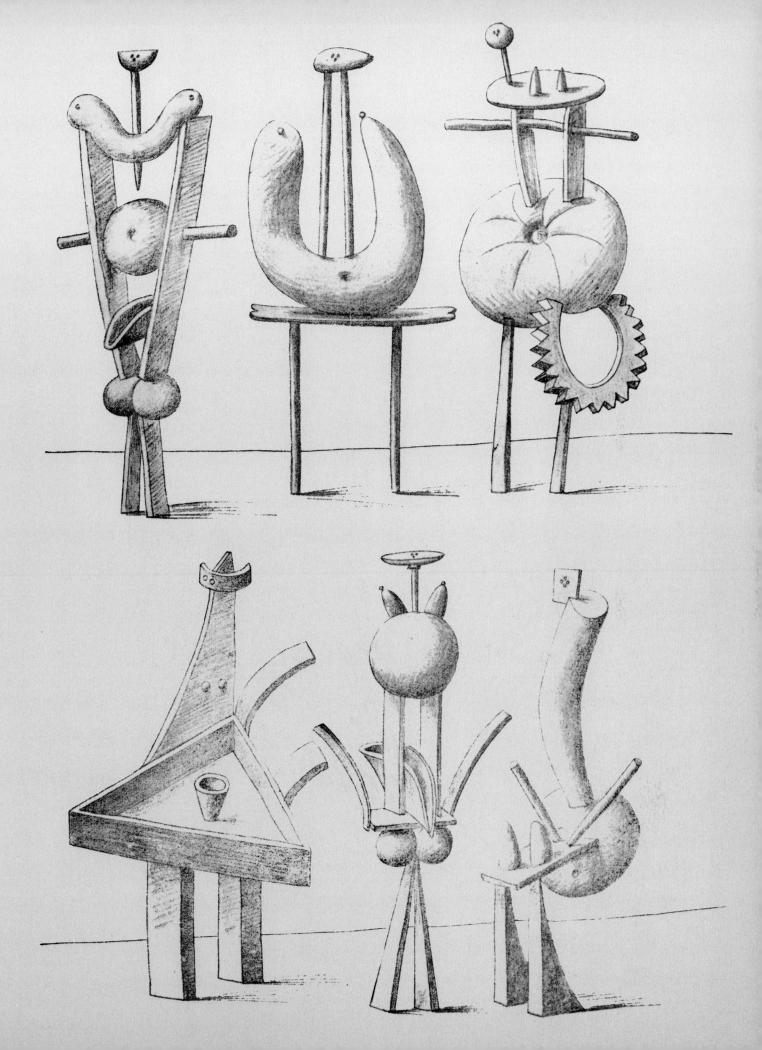

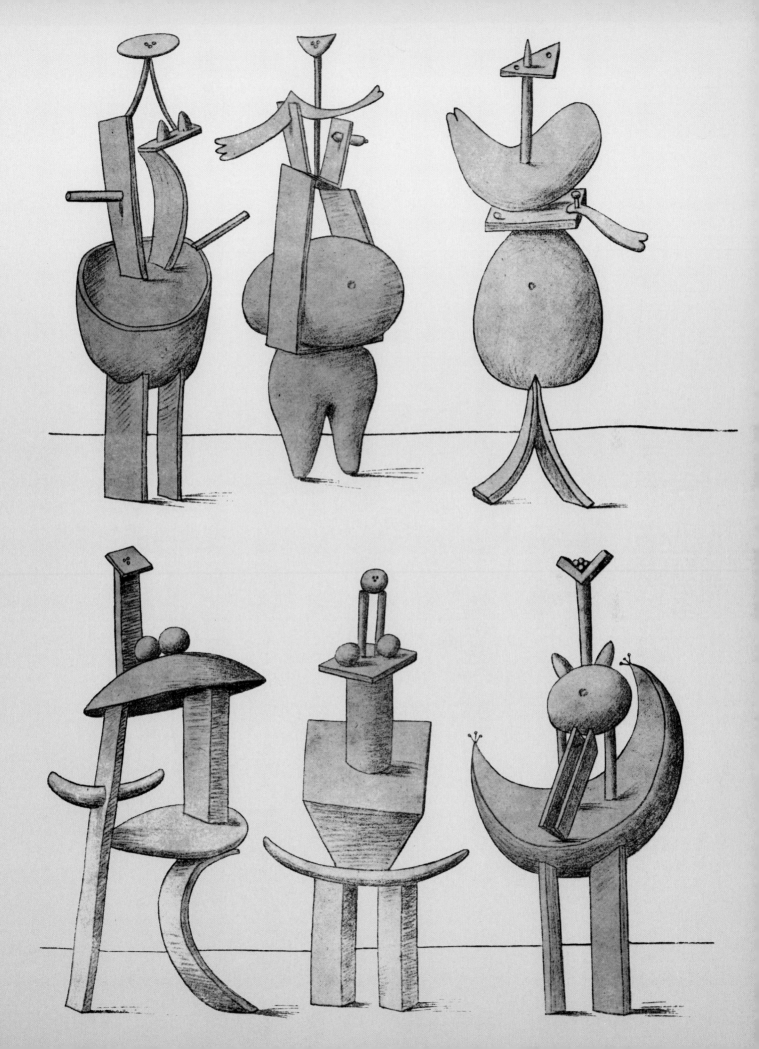

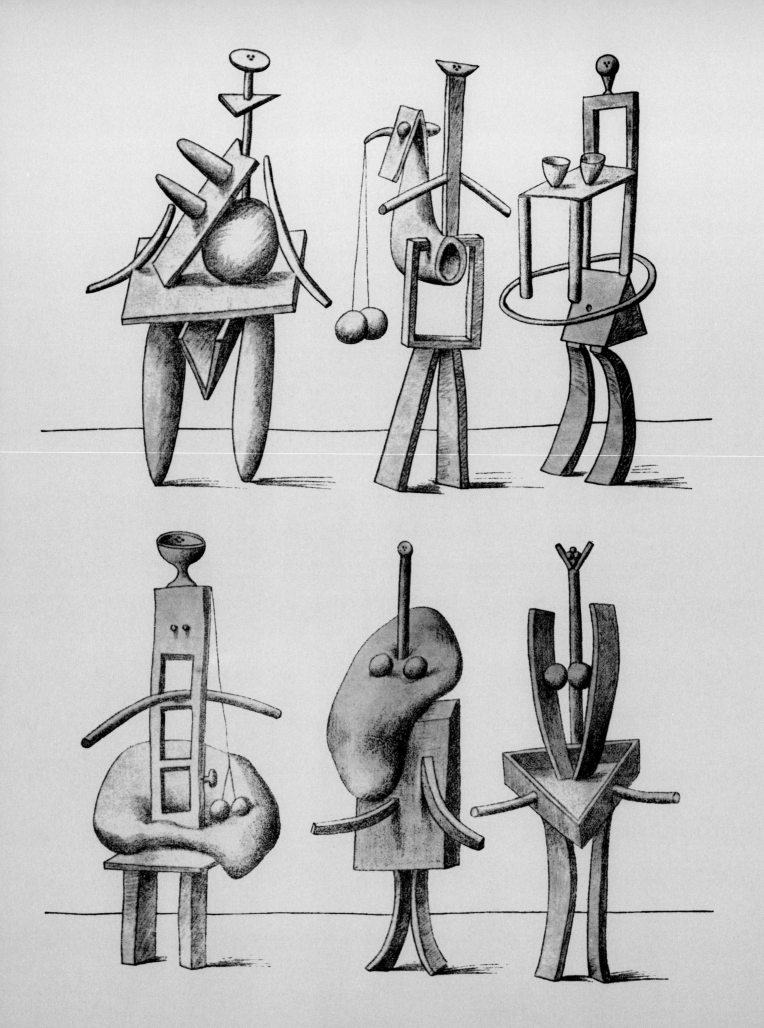

Figure 120
Picasso holding Maya
late 1936

takes on various semiabstract attributes: some of these figures have become walking phalluses; others are tables, moons, bowls, wedges of cheese, tomatoes, gameboards. Arms are pegs, boards, gears, long-legged insects. Picasso called this series *An Anatomy*; he published it in the first number of the surrealist journal *Minotaure*. It constitutes a dictionary of the expressive forms that he used to depict the female body and fore-shadows the visual lexicon that he developed in creating the faces of the weeping women.

Picasso briefly devoted himself to setting up a semiconjugal household with Walter. He had been profoundly moved by Maya's birth and was at least initially a dutiful father (figs. 120–21), changing her, washing her, and playing with her.[39] On 27 March 1936 he traveled to

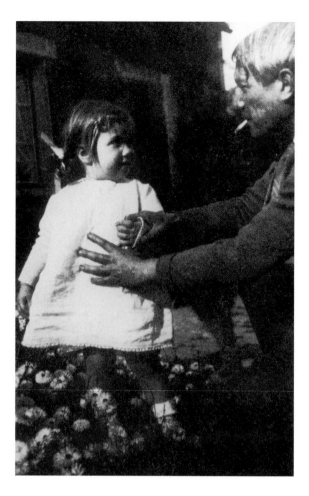

Figure 121
Picasso and Maya
Tremblay-sur-Mauldre
February–March 1937

Juan-les-Pins with Walter and Maya for a six-week vacation. It was the most extended effort Picasso made to establish a domestic environment with Walter; it was also the last. Picasso "did not want me to laugh," recalled Walter. "He was always telling me: be serious!"[40] His dissatisfactions—particularly his frustrations with her limited abilities and intelligence—were apparently heightened during this trip. Upon studying photographs from the Juan-les-Pins stay, Walter said, "You see, he was bored!"[41]

Bored perhaps, but distracted too. By 1936 Picasso's depictions of Walter had shifted from being dual explorations of her personality and sensuality to straightforward recordings of her character. *Woman in an Orange Straw Hat* (fig. 122) is a typical 1936 portrait of Walter. Depicted in profile, she wears a festive blouse and hat. Picasso uses strong tones of orange, green, and purple to animate the portrait. Her

Figure 122
*Woman in an
Orange Straw Hat*
1936
Oil on canvas
18 x 15 in.
(45.7 x 38.1 cm)
Beatrice and Philip Gersh

eyes avoid ours as well as Picasso's, both here and in a contemporary photograph of her taken by the artist (fig. 123).

By the time Picasso painted this portrait, he already had met Dora Maar. He is said to have first spotted her in the Café des Deux Magots in January 1936. Eluard had introduced them by March, but Picasso did not instantly embark on a close relationship with her.

Figure 123
Marie-Thérèse Walter
with Maya
Juan-les-Pins
April 1936
Photographed by Picasso

During February he had a short-lived liason with Alice Paalen, wife of artist Wolfgang Paalen. During a summer 1936 trip to Mougins, on which Maar accompanied Picasso, it appears that he had a brief affair with Nusch Eluard, tacitly approved by her husband. Nevertheless Maar became Picasso's dedicated mistress; by late 1936 she was firmly entrenched in his life and had essentially uprooted Walter.

"It must be painful," Picasso told John Richardson, "for a girl to see in a painting that she is on the way out."[42] Walter indeed recognized this by 1936, although her relationship with Picasso diminished slowly over the following fifteen years. Picasso saw her regularly on Thursdays and Sundays, days when Maya was not in school. Between 1936 and 1940 Walter and Maya were resident in Tremblay-sur-Mauldre, staying at a farmhouse owned by one of Picasso's first dealers, Ambroise Vollard. Picasso maintained a studio at the Tremblay house and intermittently worked there during visits to the pair. He continued to write affectionate letters to Walter and Maya.[43] Walter wrote Picasso often; 935 of her letters are now in the archives of the Musée Picasso in Paris.

"One's work is sort of a diary," Picasso (fig. 124) observed, and he dated his works so that they would provide documentation for a future scientific analysis.[44] The perambulations that his depictions of women took in the late 1920s and early 1930s consequently may be meticulously charted. Their dramatic emotional content provided fertile territory for Picasso when he was searching for metaphors to express the intensity of his feelings over events in Spain. The weeping women were

Figure 124
Picasso
Paris
1935

the outgrowth of his emotive renderings of Koklova and Walter and also reflect his then-current relationship with Dora Maar. All three women, with their varied personalities, were the muses for Picasso's creation of the weeping women, which are, in effect, superimposed pages from his visual diary.

Notes

1. Simone de Beauvoir, *The Second Sex,* trans. H.M. Parshley (New York: Vintage Books, 1989), 182. First published in France in 1949.

2. Quoted in Lord 1993, 123.

3. Gedo 1980A, and Huffington 1988, for example.

4. Richardson 1991, 310, 318, for example, cites her efforts to distance Picasso from surrealist poet and painter Max Jacob because she did not find Jacob respectable, and her fury over the publication of Fernande Olivier's memoirs of Olivier's early years as Picasso's mistress.

5. Cooper 1976, n.p.

6. Daix 1993, 166, says that Picasso had Eugenia Erraturiz assume the role of "intimate counselor."

7. *"Ma pauvre Eva est morte....Ca a été une grande douleur pour moi et je sais que vous le regretterez. Elle a toujours été si bonne pour moi."* Letter of 8 January 1916, Gertrude Stein Archives, Beinecke Rare Book and Manuscript Library, Yale University. Trans. in Daix 1993, 147.

8. On Picasso's affair with Gabrielle (Gaby) Lespinasse (at the time of his relationship with her she was Gabrielle Depeyre), see Richardson 1987, and Klüver and Martin 1989, 72.

9. Penrose 1981A, 219.

10. Gilot and Lake 1964, 147–48.

11. Ibid., 149.

12. These abstract drawings, thought to be studies for Picasso's illustrations for Balzac's *Chef-d'oeuvre inconnu* (Paris: Ambroise Vollard, 1931), appear in at least three 1924 notebooks. See nos. 83–85 in Glimcher and Glimcher 1986.

13. Richardson 1991, 1, 5.

14. Lawrence Gowing, in the context of his overall linkage of this painting to crucifixions, related this figure to Donatello's *Weeping Maenad at the Cross,* one of the San Lorenzo pulpits. Gowing, "Two Notable Acquisitions," *The Tate Gallery Annual Report 1964–65* (London: Tate Gallery, 1966), 10–11. See also Alley 1986, 15. For an account of the various possible interpretations of this figure, see Gasman 1981, 631-32.

15. See John Golding, "Picasso and Surrealism," repr. in Penrose and Golding 1973, 57–60.

16. *The Three Dancers* was reproduced in *La Révolution surréaliste* 4 (15 July 1925): 17.

17. Penrose 1981A, 256. Brassaï described Picasso's La Boëtie residence, contrasting his congested studio with the apartment in which Picasso and Koklova lived: "Not the least hint of casualness, not a grain of dust. Polished, gleaming floors and furniture." Quoted in Daix 1993, 193.

18. Gilot and Lake 1964, 325.

19. Quoted in Parmelin 1966, 91.

20. Gasman 1981, 1154, for example.

21. Ibid., 1152–53. Koklova had developed psychosomatic disturbances manifested by grinning and extending her tongue.

22. There is some debate over the date of Picasso and Walter's first encounter. Schwarz argues that they must have met in 1925; Jean Boggs (in Cleveland 1992, 224, note 3) speculates on a first meeting in 1926.

23. Daix 1993, 202. In February 1974 Pierre Cabanne interviewed Walter and recounts a slightly different version of the same meeting. She recalled: *"J'avais 17 ans passés, j'allais faire des courses sur les boulevards. J'allais acheter un petit col. Il m'a regardée. Il avait une superbe cravate, rouge et noire, que j'ai encore d'ailleurs. Il m'a fait un beau sourire. Puis il m'a abordée et il m'a dit: 'Mademoiselle, vous avez un visage intéressant. Je voudrais faire votre portrait.' Il a ajouté: 'Je sens que nous ferons de grandes choses ensemble.' C'était le samedi 8 janvier 1927, il*

était six heures du soir. Et puis, ma foi, il m'a dit: 'Je suis Picasso.'" ("I was 17 years old, I was walking on the boulevard. I had bought a blouse with a Peter Pan collar. He saw me. He had a superb red and black tie, moreover. He gave me a big smile. Then he approached me and said, 'Mademoiselle, you have an interesting face. I would like to do your portrait.' He added, 'I think that we will do great things together.' This was Saturday, 8 January 1927, it was six o'clock in the evening. And then, to be sure, he said to me, 'I am Picasso.'"). Walter, interviewed in Cabanne 1974, 2; see also Cabanne 1975 (II) 245; and Gasman 1981, 954.

24. Barr never mentioned Walter; even Penrose (1981A, 269) only minimally acknowledges her. For an in-depth study of Picasso's "MT" paintings, see Gasman 1981, 913–77; Daix 1983; and Gopnik 1981/82. Walter told Gasman that Picasso continued the practice of drawing their initials for many years as a token of his affection for her; Gasman 1981, 965.
25. Walter interview in Gasman 1981, 64, 318.
26. Walter interview, ibid., 64 and note 2.
27. It was Robert Rosenblum who first linked Picasso's late 1920s nudes with erectile tissue; see Rosenblum, "Picasso and the Anatomy of Eroticism," in Schiff 1976, 77.

28. Picasso to Zervos in 1929; quoted by Richardson, "Picasso and Marie-Thérèse Walter," in New York 1985, n.p. [6].
29. Berger 1965, 156-57. Rosenblum 1966, 24-26, similarly interpreted *Nude on a Black Couch*: "In [this] image of sleep, the release occurs in a subconscious realm; for the body now seems deprived of material substance, while neverthe-less retaining the rounded fullness of female fertility. This descent below consciousness is achieved by pictorial puns which may depend ultimately on the visual double entendres of Cubism, but which exist here in an anti-intellectual realm of erotic magic that stands as one of the highpoints of surrealist poetry. Thus, night, love, and procreation are suggested by the hair, which also becomes a kind of seed that just touches an ovarian breast; by the green stem and white flower that grow from a hand relaxed in sleep; by the crescent-moon shape of a closed eye; or by the philodendrons that, newly nurtured by the orange-red heat of dawn just visible through the window, rise from the protective, uterine folds of black couch and lavender flesh."
30. The significance of Picasso's use of color is explored in depth in Nochlin 1980.
31. Picasso to André Malraux, quoted in Malraux, *La Tête d'obsidi-enne*. Paris: Gallimard, 1974.
32. Richardson 1985B, 66.
33. Gasman 1981, 1432.
34. Walter interview with Gasman; ibid., 1443-44.
35. Richardson 1985B, 67.
36. Duncan 1961, III.
37. Stein 1970, 82–83. Stein exaggerated in retrospect when she declared that Picasso did not work for two years, as it was clear that this period lasted for several months.

38. See, for example, the poem of 24–28 November 1935, which begins *"lengua de fuego abanica su cara en la flauta la copa..."* (tongue of fire fans its face in the flute the cup). Picasso 1989, 46.
39. Cabanne 1975 (II), 276, based on the author's discussions with Walter.
40. Walter interview in Gasman 1981, 60.
41. Walter interview, ibid., 1190.
42. Richardson 1985B, 68.
43. Several of these are published in Tokyo 1981.
44. Picasso in an interview with E. Tériade, in *L'Intransigéant*, 15 June 1932. Quoted in Brassaï 1964, 97.

"*...the gift*

of metamorphosis.

"One day I take the saddle and the handlebars.

I put them one on top of the other, and I make

a bull's head. All well and good. But what I

should have done straight after was to throw away

the bull's head. Throw it into the street, into the

gutter, anywhere, but throw it away. Then a

workman comes along. He picks it up. He thinks

that with this bull's head he could perhaps make

a saddle and a set of bicycle handlebars. And he

does it....That would have been magnificent.

It is the gift of metamorphosis."

—Pablo Picasso[1]

*T*o date surprisingly little has been written about the details of Picasso's relationship with Dora Maar.[2] Legend has it that Picasso spotted her at the Café des Deux Magots, where she was alone, throwing a sharp penknife down between her fingers into a wooden table.[3] Subsequently Picasso asked Eluard to introduce him, and their relationship began shortly thereafter. During the summer of 1936 she joined Picasso in Mougins, where he had taken up residence with the Eluards, Roland and Valentine Penrose, Christian and Yvonne Zervos, Man Ray and his companion, Ady, and Man Ray's former student Lee Miller. She already knew most of this group through her own career as a photographer and had photographed them when they visited Picasso in Boisgeloup in March 1936.[4]

Picasso often spoke of chronicling the metamorphosis of his paintings by having them photographed in process.[5] Maar was a relatively sophisticated photographer, having been associated with the surrealists since the early 1930s. She had exhibited with them in Tenerife in 1935 and in the International Surrealist Exhibition in London in 1936. Around the neck of Marcel Jean's 1936 sculpture *The Specter of the Gardenia* (fig. 125) is a piece from an unfinished film in which she appears, made by filmmaker Louis Chavance.

Maar shared a darkroom with Brassaï for a brief period. She lived with Chavance and then the writer Georges Bataille in the early 1930s.[6] As a result she was acutely aware of the political efforts of Bataille's left-wing group Contre-Attaque; she signed their manifestos and attended their meetings. Previously she had been active in an anti-Fascist group, "Appel à la lutte" (Call to arms). When Picasso was searching for a studio at the end of 1936, Maar suggested 7, rue des Grands-Augustins, a building with which she was well acquainted because it housed the meetings of Contre-Attaque.

Maar was born Henrietta Théodora Markovitch in Tours in 1907.[7] Her father was a Jewish Yugoslav architect; her mother was French Catholic. She spent several years of her childhood in Argentina,

Page 172: detail
Woman Dressing Her Hair
(Figure 141)

CHAPTER **V**

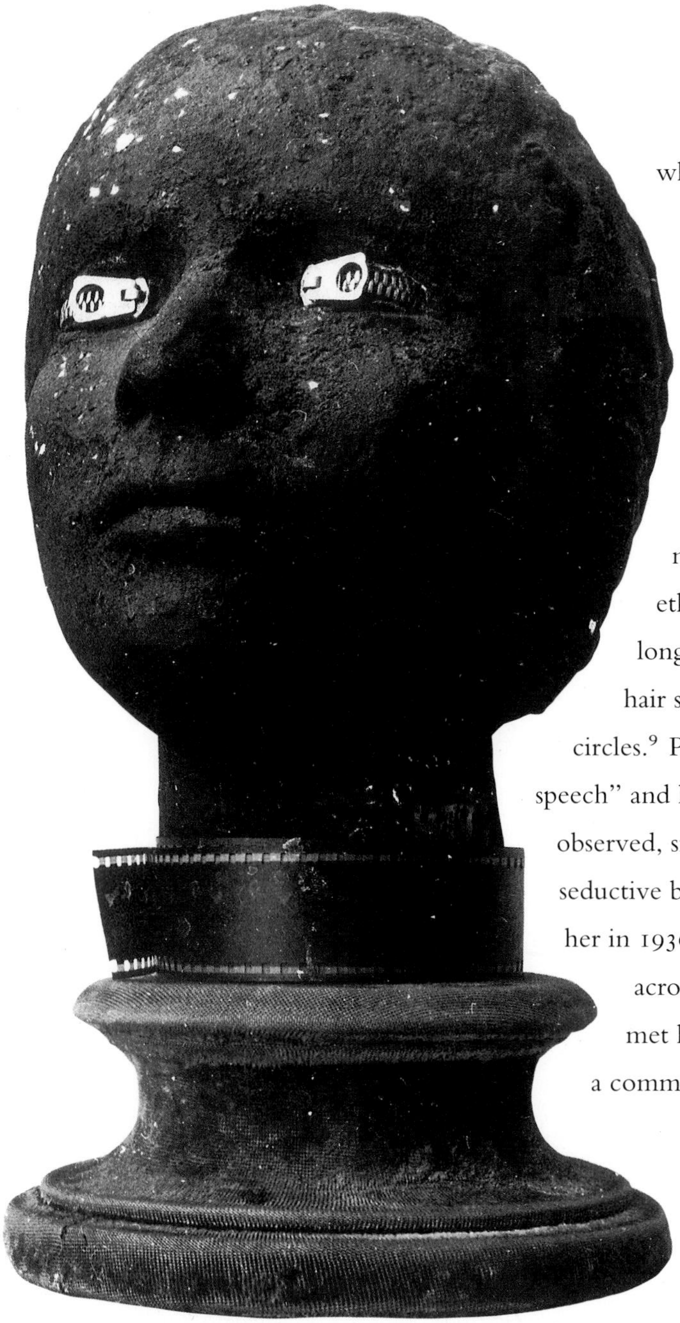

Figure 125
Marcel Jean
The Specter of the Gardenia
1936
Plaster with painted black
cloth, zippers, and strip
of movie film on velvet-
covered wood base
13 ⅞ x 7 x 9 ⅞ in.
(35.2 x 25.1 cm)
The Museum of Modern
Art, New York, D. and J.
de Menil Fund

where she became fluent in Spanish and demonstrated an aptitude for foreign languages.[8] She studied painting formally, first at the Ecole des Arts Décoratifs, then at the Académie Passy, and finally at the Académie Julian with André Lhote.

Early in life she changed her name to Dora Maar, a more exotic, less ethnic appellation. This, along with her long, red fingernails and unpredictable hair styles, attracted attention in surrealist circles.[9] Penrose noted her "quick decisive speech" and her "low-pitched voice"; both were, he observed, signs of character.[10] Maar clearly had a seductive beauty when Man Ray photographed her in 1936 with her fingers draped prominently across her forehead (fig. 126). When Picasso met her she had a powerful sense of self and a commanding presence.

The Spanish Civil War began when Picasso and Maar were in Mougins. Maar impressed Picasso by discoursing at length on the politics of the situation. Upon their return to Paris Maar helped Picasso find a new apartment; she remained in her own place on the rue d'Astorg. Just before the Occupation Maar moved into an apartment on the rue de Savoie, around the corner from Picasso's studio.

Picasso made several separate portraits of Walter and Maar early in 1937. Each is seated in the same type of chair; each rests a hand alongside her head. Walter (fig. 127) appears in a vivid, striped dress and matching hat. She seems a youthful, elegant beauty, pleasant but not

Figure 126
Dora Maar
1936
Photographed by
Man Ray

powerful. Maar (fig. 128) is painted in more acidic colors. Her eyes stare intently, confronting the viewer; heavy makeup accents her cheeks and lips. The red nails against the dark black hair bespeak a strong, assertive woman. The prominent eyes outlined with dark strokes and the tufted bangs characterize other portraits of her. In one from November 1937 (fig. 129) she appears in a room with intensely colored walls. Even without the buttressing of an armchair hers is a powerful presence.

Maar was an active participant in Picasso's life and is generally credited with heightening his awareness of political causes. She was actively involved in the conception and execution of *Guernica* as well, painting the hairs on the horse and documenting the mural's progress.[11] Yet for all her intelligence, Maar had to contend with Picasso's past. He was still married to Koklova; he had fathered Walter's child and saw Walter and Maya regularly once or twice a week. Maar often encountered these women—as would Françoise Gilot nearly a decade later—and interacted with them. Gilot quoted Picasso telling a story:

"I remember one day while I was painting Guernica *in the big studio in the Rue des Grands-Augustins, Dora Maar was with me. Marie-Thérèse dropped in and when she found Dora there, she grew angry and said to her, 'I have a child by this man. It's my place to be here with him. You can leave right now.' Dora said, 'I have as much reason as you have to be here. I haven't borne him a child but I don't see what difference that makes.' I kept on painting and they kept on arguing. Finally Marie-Thérèse turned to me and said, 'Make up your mind. Which one of us goes?' It was a hard decision to make. I liked them both, for different reasons: Marie-Thérèse because she was sweet and gentle and did whatever I wanted her to, and Dora because she was intelligent. I decided I had no interest in making a decision. I was satisfied with things as they were. I told them they'd have to fight it out themselves. So they began to wrestle. It's one of my choicest memories."*[12]

If true, this incident took place in May, or at the latest June, of 1937, around the time when Picasso was completing *Guernica* and beginning

Figure 127
(page 178)
Seated Woman (Portrait of Marie-Thérèse Walter)
6 January 1937
Oil on canvas
39 ³/₈ x 31 ⁷/₈ in.
(100 x 81 cm)
Musée Picasso, Paris
(MP 159)

Figure 128
(page 179)
Portrait of Dora Maar
1937
Oil on canvas
36 ¹/₄ x 25 ⁵/₈ in.
(92 x 65 cm)
Musée Picasso, Paris
(MP 158)

Figure 129
Portrait of Dora Maar
23 November 1937
Oil on canvas
21 ¾ x 18 ¼ in.
(55.3 x 46.3 cm)
Musée Picasso, Paris
(MP 166)

Figure 130
Dora Maar, Mougins
1937
Photographed by
Lee Miller

Figure 131
Dora Maar, Picasso, and
Lee Miller at Mougins
1937

work on the weeping women postscripts. Both Walter and Maar were unhappy; Walter especially sought exclusivity, while Maar did not want to be mired among estranged wives and former mistresses. She would secretly visit Tremblay, where Walter and Maya were residing: "[Vollard] loaned the house to Picasso, who installed his mistress there, the woman he knew before me, Marie-Thérèse, with their daughter, Maya. And he used to go out there often for weekends, leaving me alone in Paris. Sometimes I would take a taxi there. To see what I could see. Nothing. And yet behind those walls I knew Picasso was there with her and the little girl. Oh, he made no secret of it...."[13]

Concurrently Maar witnessed her own pictorial deformation in Picasso's work. An August holiday in Mougins (figs. 130–31) with Picasso and their friends proved tranquil and enjoyable to Maar, but she was already aware of the awesome power of Picasso's personality. Years later she recalled, "Sometimes he would exclaim, 'I'm God, I'm God.' But then you realized that in God's presence there would never be any doubt about who He was, and you would wonder whether Picasso in reality wasn't the other one."[14] She captured Picasso's authority in a photograph (fig. 132) taken at Golfe-Juan. In the ensuing months Picasso's portraits of her became more grotesque. In two (figs. 133–34) the hat and the armchair provide a framework for Picasso to create netted structures around her; she is engulfed by these webs and in essence is trapped within them. Her eyes are transfigured into a tilted cup and saucer, her nostrils two large snouts, her lips a jagged blade. In a third (fig. 135) her face is lathered with paint. Her eyes, brows, and lashes are traced in red, while ochre, green, and pink swirls decorate her cheeks. In a number of paintings from 1938 and 1939 she is encased in

Figure 132
Picasso at Golfe-Juan,
1937
Photographed by
Dora Maar

Figure 133
(page 182)
Seated Woman
27 April 1938
Ink, gouache, and chalk
on paper
30 1/8 x 21 5/8 in.
(76.5 x 55 cm)
Ernst Beyeler, Basel

Figure 134
(page 183)
*Dora Maar Seated
in a Wicker Chair*
29 April 1938
Ink, pastel, and wash on
paper
30 1/8 x 21 3/4 in.
(76.5 x 55.2 cm)
The Jacques and Natasha
Gelman Collection

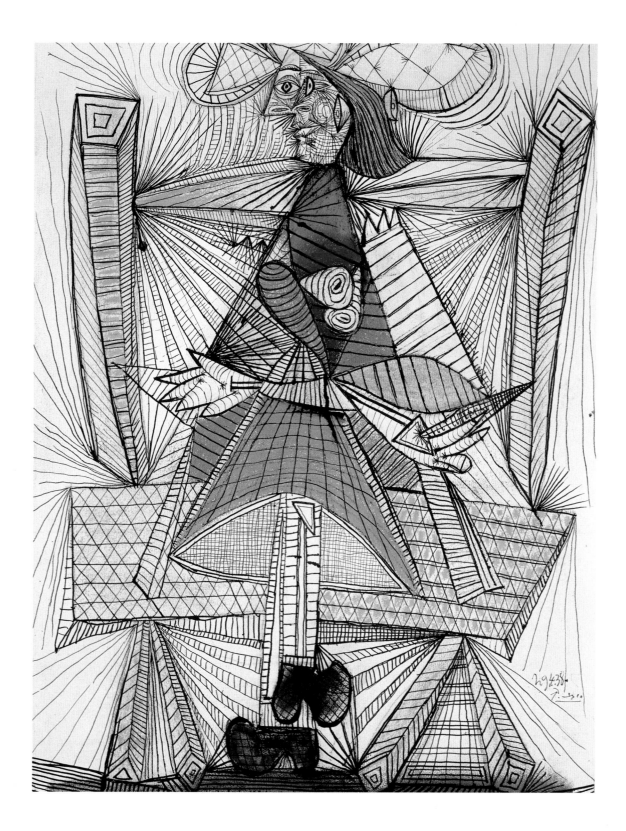

Figure 135

Woman with a Hairnet

1938

Oil on canvas

25 5/8 x 21 1/4 in.

(65.1 x 54 cm)

Picasso estate

(no. 12829),

Marina Picasso

Collection,

private collection

Figure 136

The Yellow Sweater

31 October 1939

Oil on canvas

31 7/8 x 25 5/8 in.

(81 x 65 cm)

The Berggruen

Collection, on loan to

The National Gallery,

London

coiled basketwork. In one example her body only is covered by such a
mesh (fig. 136); in another (fig. 137) she is consumed completely by
these coils. The result is a monstrous, faceless being that appears less
menacing than entrapped. Both the "basketwork" women and the
women in webs seem locked within themselves, either through external
elements or through their own wrappings. Perhaps these were metaphors
for Picasso's perceptions of Maar's self-absorption and mood swings.

The events of 1939 encroached on Picasso and Maar. Picasso's mother died in January. Spain fell to Franco's forces in March; the Germans invaded Czechoslovakia that month. Picasso and Maar traveled to Antibes for the summer; Walter and Maya were sent to Royan, on the southwestern coast of France, but the tide of daily events did not escape them either.

Picasso wrote to Walter on July 19: "My Love, My Love, My Love: I want you to be happy, and to think only of being happy. I would give anything for that to be so....My own tears would mean

Figure 137

Seated Woman with a Hat
10 September 1938
Oil and sand on wood
21 ⁵/₈ x 18 ¹/₈ in.
(54.9 x 46 cm)
The Menil Collection,
Houston

Figure 138

Woman with a Straw Hat
in Front of a Flowered
Background
25 June 1938
Oil on canvas
28 ¾ x 23 ⅝ in.
(73 x 60 cm)
Picasso estate

nothing to me, if I could stop you from shedding even one more."[15] His
paintings of Walter from 1938 and 1939 show a more mature woman
still surrounded by symbols of her fecundity and femininity (fig. 138).
These were dramatically different from contemporary depictions of Maar.

Devastated by the failure of the causes in which she believed,
Maar by 1939 was swept into a tide of pessimism and despair. In *Woman*

Reclining on a Couch Maar's face is an elongated, jagged shape (fig 139). Face, neck, and breast all unite in an irregular profile; her body is subsumed by cubist forms. A palette—perhaps Picasso's, perhaps Maar's (for by this time she was painting)—hangs beside her head on the wall. She stares out at the viewer with alarm. The painting supports the notion that by this time Maar had become increasingly terrified, preoccupied with events, and despite her own forceful nature heavily dependent on Picasso.

Figure 139
*Woman Reclining
on a Couch*
21 January 1939
Oil on canvas
38 ½ x 51 in.
(97.8 x 130 cm)
Private collection

Figure 140

Night Fishing at Antibes

August 1939

Oil on canvas

81 x 125 in.

(205.7 x 317.5 cm)

The Museum of Modern

Art, New York, Mrs.

Simon Guggenheim

Fund, 1952

In August he painted *Night Fishing at Antibes* (fig. 140), a work loosely referring to contemporary events in France.[16] The scene features an elongated Maar on the right holding the handlebars of a bicycle, with Breton's wife, Jacqueline Lamba, in a green skirt next to her. The elegantly clad women stand on a jetty watching the men haul in the evening's catch. The youthful fisherman in the center suggests a playful, lighthearted gathering, but this impression is immediately contradicted by the darkness of the setting and the shadows that engulf nearly all of its

figures. The contrast is menacing, suggestive of equally alarming current events in France.

Night Fishing at Antibes was painted during Picasso's last summer before the Occupation of Paris. From Antibes he traveled back to Paris and then almost immediately headed with Maar to Royan; although overtaken by German troops, it was still a relatively easy place for him to work, as the German presence was rather low-key.[17] There he began his largest portrait of Maar: Woman Dressing Her Hair (fig. 141). This figure is a composite of many of the ideograms found in the weeping women, though not the tears. She may also be read as a fleshy version of one of the Anatomy figures. Her face is cleaved down the middle, a modification of Picasso's double portrait format, earlier seen in a 1931 image of Walter (fig. 116). Her chunky feet resemble giant mitts. Her breasts are splayed and possess a phallic aspect. The right arm becomes a sword; the left belongs to an automaton. This portrait, occurring as it does toward the end of a series of double portraits of Maar, provides a full-length picture of the distress that Maar, here symbolizing all women in wartime, was experiencing. It is a simplified version of the contemporaneous gouache of Maar completely losing all composure (fig. 142), trapped in a web of patterned lines. This woman—an evocation of Maar's agitated state of mind at the time—pulls at her hair and seems to have begun unraveling.

In 1941 Picasso, residing in Paris, was busy writing his play Desire Caught by the Tail.[18] For one of his protagonists, Big Foot, Picasso wrote: "Fear of the moodiness of love and the moods of the caperings of rage. Gargle of the molten metal of her hair shrieking with pain all her joy at being possessed....The reflection of her grimaces painted on the mirror which is open to all the winds aromatizes the hardness of her blood on the coldness of the flight of doves which receives it."[19] This could be a description of Maar; she had in the Royan and Paris portraits (figs. 133–37, for example) been transformed into a distorted version of herself. Portraits from 1940–41 (figs. 143–44) also present her as misshapen. Her features are distended; seen in profile and frontally in Picasso's double portrait format, her eyes bulge, their

Figure 141
Woman Dressing Her Hair
June 1940
Oil on canvas
51 ¼ x 38 ¼ in.
(130.2 x 97.2 cm)
Mrs. Bertram Smith,
New York

Figure 142

Figure 142
Portrait of Dora Maar
30 December 1939
Gouache on paper
18 ⅛ x 15 in.
(46 x 38 cm)
Private collection

lashes metamorphosed into teardrops. Her nostrils are swollen, her lips are immense packets of flesh that do not align. Her armchair is rickety, a fragile, wiry structure that frames her body. She is a woman literally coming apart.

When Picasso painted his last substantial portrait of Dora Maar in October 1942 (fig. 145), he departed completely from the ideogrammatic features that he had heretofore used to describe her. This is a more conventional, frontal portrait of her in a simple orange-and-green-striped dress, with shoulder-length black hair, staring out at the viewer.[20] It is a revelatory document of a woman shattered by the turbulent events of the time. Her face is entirely intact. She is no longer deconstructed, shattered, or masked; now she is quite legible and accessible, staring vacantly at the viewer. The emotion displayed on her face tells its own story.

Though he would not meet Françoise Gilot until May of 1943, there was already tension between Picasso and Maar. This was due in

Figure 143
Head of a Woman
11 January 1940
Gouache on paper
mounted on board
18 ⅛ x 15 in.
(46 x 38 cm)
Private collection,
England

Figure 144

Woman in an Armchair

1941/44

Oil on canvas

45 ¼ x 34 ¾ in.

(114.9 x 88.3 cm)

Morton G. Neumann

Family Collection,

Chicago

Figure 145

Portrait of Dora Maar
9 October 1942
Oil on canvas
36 ¼ x 28 ¾ in.
(92.1 x 73 cm)
Stephen Hahn
Collection,
New York

part to the wartime conditions under which they were forced to live as well as to the conflicts that naturally arose between these two strong-willed personalities. It is worth speculating how (and why) Maar was protected from the Germans and what role Picasso played in securing her safety. Under such pressures, and confronted eventually by the reality of Gilot's presence in Picasso's life, Maar reportedly began to have hallucinations and uncontrollable public outbursts. According to James Lord, who served as Maar's confidant and companion in the late 1940s and early 1950s, she had suffered a nervous breakdown:

One day she was found sitting naked in the stairway of her apartment building, to the consternation of a wedding party coming down from an upper floor. And then there was an appalling outburst of hysteria in a movie theatre, the police were summoned, and she was taken to the psychiatric hospital of Sainte-Anne in the fourteenth arrondissement....She was subjected to a series of electroshock treatments, not unlike artificially induced epileptic convulsions, better left undescribed. Eluard was outraged and insisted Picasso do something. Jacques Lacan, a friend of all of them and already an eminent psycho-analyst...was enlisted to help [in 1945]. He got Dora out of the madhouse and put her in a private clinic. Later she underwent analysis with him.[21]

"For me, [Dora Maar] is the weeping woman," declared Picasso. "For years I gave her a tortured appearance, not out of sadism, and without any pleasure on my part, but in obedience to a vision that had imposed itself on me."[22]

"My entire life has been, because of him," remarked Marie-Thérèse Walter, "full of happiness, then of tears. Of tears above all....He was a wonderfully terrible man."[23]

Elements of both women and of Olga Koklova appear as the ideograms constituting the weeping women of the momentous year of

1937; their features become the monstrous eyes, noses, teeth, mouths, and ears of these symbolic figures. For Picasso the actualities of these women's lives as they were entwined with his merged with the events of his time and his evolving visual vocabulary to create riveting images of shock, terror, and despair. The weeping women provide striking evidence that Picasso discarded nothing from his private life but instead harnessed all of its elements for the powerful expression of themes both personal and universal.

Picasso too was not above weeping; Maar recalled discovering him once, crying in his studio. "Asked why he was crying, he replied that it was impossible to explain save by saying 'Life is too terrible. Life is too terrible.'"[24]

The weeping women stand at the intersection of Picasso's personal and political passions. Here he embodied the agonies of his native Spain, Europe, and the world in general, yet in their features the weeping women also encapsulated Picasso's anger toward Olga Koklova, his response to an overwrought Marie-Thérèse Walter, and the emotional intensity of Dora Maar. In assessing the individual components of the weeping women, we find evidence of Picasso's hand moving over the most minute aspects of each face. The strokes of his hand mirrored the thoughts in his mind; they provide insights into his shifting attitudes on a daily, sometimes hourly, basis. His later portraits of women would be far more restrained, an avenue for mostly stylistic experimentation. For a brief period in 1937 Picasso found in the weeping women an ideal vehicle by which he could express the raging emotions of the day.

Notes

1. In Parmelin 1966, 76–77.

2. I am grateful to Dora Maar, who, during my stay in Paris in May 1992, discussed various aspects of her years with Picasso. The sole volume on her life is the recent one by James Lord (Lord 1993), which focuses on the 1940s and 1950s. Lord reports, 167–68, that Maar kept a journal; to date it has not been seen by scholars.

3. Marcel Jean (interview with the author, February 1992) recalled that he had heard that Maar seduced Picasso by giving him her gloves at the Deux Magots.

4. Penrose 1981B, 69.

5. "It would be very interesting to preserve photographically, not the stages, but the metamorphoses of a picture." Picasso to Christian Zervos; in Zervos 1935, 174; translated in Barr 1946, 272.

6. Marcel Jean, interview with the author, February 1992.

7. Her birthdate has recently been given by Lord as 22 November 1907. Lord 1993, 169.

8. Maar speaks English fluently.

9. Marcel Jean, interview with the author, February 1992.

10. Penrose 1981A, 289. Both were still evident when I spoke with her in 1992. See also Lord 1993, 63, 95 ("the exquisite birdsong quiver of her voice, unique, an enchantment"), 169, 207.

11. Richardson 1980, 19. See also Lord 1993, 159.

12. Gilot 1990, 210–11.

13. Lord 1993, 128.

14. Ibid., 122.

15. Picasso to Walter, postmarked 19 July 1939, Antibes. Published in Tokyo 1981, 119.

16. See Burgard 1986, 657–72.

17. On Picasso during the Occupation, see Goggin 1985, Cone 1992, and Dorléac 1993.

18. This play, in which Maar participated, was staged as a reading by Louise and Michel Leiris in 1944.

19. Picasso 1950, 45.

20. Ironically, Lord recounted a hitherto unknown story told by Maar: that this portrait was painted by Picasso over a portrait by Jean Cocteau of Maar, which Picasso had commissioned from him. See Lord 1993, 121–22.

21. Ibid., 101–2. For further details see Crespelle 1969, 173–74.

22. Quoted in Crespelle 1969, 153.

23. *"Ma vie entière a été, à cause de lui, de bonheur, puis de pleurs. De pleurs surtout….C'était un homme merveilleusement terrible."* Walter to Cabanne, quoted in Cabanne 1974, 10.

24. Lord 1993, 144.

Acknowledgments

*T*his project has been a longstanding ambition of mine. It is impossible to be a bona fide historian of twentieth-century art and avoid writing on Pablo Picasso, whose presence permeates every nook and cranny of the field. I am grateful to the Los Angeles County Museum of Art for allowing me the luxury of living in Picasso's shadow for the past three years. It has been a privilege.

Shortly after commencing work on *Picasso and the Weeping Women*, I attended the symposium on the occasion of the magnificent *Picasso & Things* exhibition organized by the Cleveland Museum of Art. At the close of three days of papers on the artist, I had a memorable conversation with Robert Rosenblum, one of the most assiduous and incisive scholars of Picasso's work. He welcomed me to the Picasso addiction and observed that, once you partake, it is almost impossible to get him out of your system. Recently Rosenblum rephrased his observation: "The amazing thing to me is his Dracula-like afterlife. Consciously or unconsciously, he arranged to have constant disclosures and excavations of work that had not been known during his lifetime. In an odd way, he has secured eternity."[1] Picasso's work alone would be sufficient to accomplish such a goal, but a coterie of devoted scholars insures it as well.

1. Quoted in Gardner 1993, 119.

Any Picasso project is considerably facilitated by the vast, ordered, and accessible resources of the Musée Picasso in Paris. Its director Gérard Regnier, its curators Hélène Lassalle, Hélène Seckel, Brigitte Léal, Anne Baldessari, and former curator Marie-Laure Bernadac, and its registrar, Paule Mazouet, have been exceptionally generous with suggestions, advice, and loans of artworks. I have spent many contented hours in the archives and comprehensive library at the Musée Picasso thanks to the tireless efforts and assistance of Laurence Berthon, Jeanne-Yvette Sudour, and Sylvie Fresnault.

Members of the Picasso family have been supportive. I am grateful to Maya Widmaier-Picasso, Olivier Widmaier-Picasso, Marina Picasso, Bernard Ruiz-Picasso, Catherine Hutin-Blay, Paloma Lopez-Cambil and Claude Ruiz-Picasso. Dora Maar has also patiently respond-

Page 198: detail
Sheet of Studies: Weeping Women
(Figure 79)

ed to my numerous questions and inquiries. I have very much appreciated their assistance and their thoughts on the exhibition's subject.

Many of the weeping women were created by Picasso as studies for or postscripts to *Guernica*, and a large number of these, now housed at the Museo Nacional Centro de Arte Reina Sofía in Madrid, were crucial to this project. I am indebted to Carmen Alborch, Spanish Minister of Culture, Felipe Vicente Garín Llombart, director, and Manuela Meña, deputy director, as well as José Luis Diez García, curator, and Teresa Fernandez de Bobadilla, conservator, of the Museo del Prado; and most especially Maria de Corral, director, Concha Goméz, and Paloma Esteban, chief curator of collections, at the Reina Sofia for their extraordinary cooperation.

Perhaps the most significant postscript to *Guernica* is the *Weeping Woman* purchased from Picasso by Roland Penrose several weeks after it was painted. This painting, now in the Tate Gallery's collection, is key to the work assembled in the exhibition. I am extremely grateful to Nicholas Serota, director of the Tate Gallery, for allowing it to appear in this context.

Many Picasso scholars have listened to my persistent questions and responded with unbridled enthusiasm for our shared fascination. I am deeply appreciative to Marie-Laure Bernadac, Jean Sutherland Boggs, the late Herschel Chipp, Dorothy Kosinski, William S. Lieberman, Marilyn McCully, Theodore Reff, Gérard Regnier, John Richardson, Robert Rosenblum, William Rubin, Werner Spies, and Ulrich Weisner for their willingness to discuss their own continuing researches. Lydia Csato Gasman was particularly generous; she shared her thoughts on Marie-Thérèse Walter and the weeping women with me over several hours in Cleveland and a long day at her home in Charlottesville, Virginia. My approach to this subject builds on Lydia Gasman's seminal work.

Midway through the organization of *Picasso and the Weeping Women*, William Rubin embarked on an exhibition devoted to Picasso's portraits. That undertaking, planned for 1996 at The Museum of Modern Art, overlaps with this one to a small degree. Mr. Rubin and I have worked to ensure that our two exhibitions do not conflict with one another. I am grateful to him for his many contributions to this project, and to Kirk Varnedoe, director of painting and sculpture at The Museum of Modern Art, for their collegial and cooperative spirit.

Other eyewitnesses, critics, and scholars have helped in myriad ways. I first met many of them in connection with my 1989 exhibition *The Dada and Surrealist Word-Image*; it was a pleasure to renew our acquaintance in this context. They include William Acquavella, Sandra Alvarez de Toledo, Alexander Apsis, Timothy Baum, Emmanuel Benador, Heinz Berggruen, Ernst Beyeler, Gilberte Brassaï, Elisa Breton, Gregory Browner, Renato Danese, Barbara Divver, Noëlle del Drago, Diana DuPont, Janis Ekdahl, Michael FitzGerald, Marcel Fleiss, Beatrice and Philip Gersh, Arnold Glimcher, Stephen Hahn, Florian Holstein, Myrtille Hugnet, Louise Izis, Maurice Jardot, Marcel Jean, Paul Josefowitz, Billy Klüver, Pamela Kort, Jan Krugier, Tzila Krugier, Ellen Kyriazi, Jean-Jacques Lebel, James Lord, Julie Martin, Isabelle Monod-Fontaine, Frederick Mulder, Jennifer Mundy, Molly Nesbit, Claudia Neugebauer, Barnett Owen, JoAnne Paradise, Klaus Perls, Antony Penrose, Patty Pfeiffer, Sandra Phillips, Eugene and Dorothy Prakapas, Lionel Prejger, Noëlle Rathier, Ruth Rattenbury, Maria Reinshagen, Claude Renouard, Sabine Rewald, Rona Roob, Angela Rosengart, Norman Rosenthal, James Snyder, MaryAnne Stevens, Michel Straus, Phyllis Tuchman, Germain Viatte, Gérard Vuilliamy, Virginia Zabriskie, and particularly John Elderfield and Jill Moser. Michael Sweeney combed the papers of Roland Penrose and Lee Miller for useful nuggets of information. Michael Findlay of Christie's assisted with loans in numerous ways in addition to twice evaluating works in the exhibition for Federal Council on the Arts and Humanities indemnification.

At a critical juncture in the planning of the exhibition and publication, PaineWebber expressed its desire to sponsor the exhibition. This is the first exhibition sponsored by PaineWebber at the Los Angeles County Museum of Art. I am honored that this project was the recipient of their exceptional largesse. My sincere thanks to Donald Marron, chairman and chief executive officer, and to Jennifer Wells, PaineWebber's curator, and to all of the people at PaineWebber for their confidence in the project and for the fortitude and financial support to allow us to realize it successfully.

The French and Spanish diplomatic corps in the United States have very kindly extended their goodwill and good offices. I would especially like to thank the Honorable Jacques Andréani, French ambassador to the United States, Gérard Coste, French consul general in Los Angeles, Jean-Claude Terrac, cultural attaché in Los Angeles, and Jacques Souilillou, cultural attaché in New York, for their assistance. The Spanish minister for cultural affairs in Washington, D.C., Dr. José Ramón Remacha, has been consistently supportive of our efforts.

We were very fortunate to have The Metropolitan Museum of Art and the Art Institute of Chicago as our partners in this venture. I was delighted to reteam with my colleagues at the Met, with whom I worked on *The Fauve Landscape*. Philippe de Montebello, William S. Lieberman, Kay Bearman, and Anne Strauss have shared many of the burdens of the exhibition. My discussions with Bill Lieberman have been especially gratifying. My appreciation is extended as well to Marukh Tarapor, Emily Rafferty, Nina Dieffenbach, Linda Sylling, Lowery Sims, J. Kent Lydecker, and Stella Paul at the Met for their efforts on behalf of the exhibition. At the Art Institute, James Wood embraced the project immediately when it was first proposed. My colleagues Charles Stuckey and Madeleine Grynstyn have provided assistance at every turn and I am grateful for their involvement. I am pleased that the exhibition will reach audiences in Los Angeles, New York, and Chicago.

Earl A. Powell III, LACMA director until 1992, resolutely supported *Picasso and the Weeping Women* from the outset. He and the board of trustees, under the presidencies of Daniel N. Belin and Robert F. Maguire III, enthusiastically encouraged its development. The project has additionally benefited from the involvement of trustees Julian Ganz,

Franklin Murphy, and Lynda Resnick. Through the museum I was fortunate to receive a grant from the Andrew W. Mellon Foundation in support of my research for this exhibition.

During the final months of the exhibition's preparation, I served as its guest curator, having departed LACMA in June 1993 to become the Joan Whitney Payson Curator at the Portland Museum of Art in Portland, Maine. I thank my colleagues there—trustees Leslie B. Otten, John J. Evans III, Rachel Armstrong, Scott M. Black, and John and Joanne Payson; and Daniel O'Leary, Jessica Nicoll, Eileen Arsenault, Kristen Leveque, and Dana Baldwin of the museum's staff— for their goodwill and patience in allowing me to lead a bicoastal existence to realize this exhibition.

At LACMA, Ronald Bratton, Elizabeth Algermissen, John Passi, Mark Mitchell, Arthur Owens, and Bill Stahl supervised and managed the tour, installation, and budget with their usual professionalism. Tom Jacobson, the museum's head of corporate support, foundations and grants, worked with me on the painstaking negotiations necessary to fund the exhibition; I am grateful to him, as well as to Lynn Terelle and Talbot Welles for their efforts. Samara Whitesides and Rachel Simon of the director's office finessed lender communications and administrative needs. Assistant registrar Chandra King, working with Renee Montgomery and Tamara Yost, capably oversaw the borrowing and return of the works of art. Joseph Fronek, Virginia Rasmussen, and Victoria Blyth-Hill performed necessary conservation work. Jessica O'Dwyer and Barbara Kraft ably coordinated the press and publicity. Mary Healy and her staff coordinated associated special events. Eleanor Hartman, Anne Diederick, John Barone, Grant Rusk, and Nancy Sutherland in the museum's library assisted in tracking obscure references and locating volumes. Maria Porges authored the accompanying brochure. Bernard Kester, the indomitable spirit of LACMA, designed the installation in Los Angeles with his usual elegant flair.

This publication is the enduring record of this exhibition. Its creation has been painful and laborious; as Picasso noted, "I am always

2. In Picasso 1964, 221.

aware that I am engaged in an activity in which the brush can accomplish what the pen cannot."[2] Nevertheless, in the end, it has been a worthwhile effort for this author. On the other hand, waiting for its completion has more than tested the patience of the museum's editor in chief Mitch Tuchman, and the volume's editor, Thomas Frick. Mr. Frick's keen intelligence and incisive queries refined the prose and considerably sharpened the contents of this volume. My writing has been enriched by his attention to detail and his dogged pursuit of perfection. It was designed by Amy McFarland, whose passion for the beautiful page and distinguished design is evident in every spread of this volume.

My colleagues in the department of twentieth-century art immediately endorsed the proposal for this exhibition. I thank Maurice Tuchman, senior curator of twentieth-century art, for his ongoing support. I am keenly appreciative of the sage counsel and unstinting friendship of Stephanie Barron, curator of twentieth-century art and acting coordinator for curatorial affairs. Howard Fox, Carol Eliel, Eric Pals, and Yvette Padilla have been helpful in various ways. I am also grateful to my colleagues in other departments of the museum, particularly Philip Conisbee, Mary Levkoff, Victor Carlson, Bruce Davis, Edward Maeder, Sheryl Conkelton, Jeffrey Cohen, and especially the late Ronald Haver.

I have been fortunate to have had several assistants who have coped with the unceasing demands of this project. Lois Sein, my dedicated volunteer for the past five years, has devoted one day every week of her life over that period to help me stay afloat. I have so appreciated her tireless efforts and her quiet efficiency. Intern Wendy Weil spent a summer tracking down lesser-known sources and building remarkable research files on subjects related to the exhibition's theme. My research assistant Margaret Tiberio, although responsible for another project, generously offered her very perceptive thoughts on this one. Grete Wolf translated hundreds of pages of German for me; Marcia Tucker provided the same service for Spanish texts. Juan José Garcia and David Britt translated Picasso's Spanish and French texts, respectively. During the final six months, Jennifer Yates capably coordinated logistical details for me at LACMA, and communicated daily as the opening drew closer. Hers was a herculean effort, one indispensable to the realization of this project.

"Youth, while we have it, we must wear daily, for it will wear away fast," commented Picasso,[3] ever mindful of his own aging as well as the fleeting youth of his children. This project has prevented me, at several junctures, from wearing my daughters daily, but I trust that Jessica and Rebecca will find something redeeming in their mother's pursuit of Picasso's intelligence. My deepest thanks to them, and to my husband Kenneth Slade above all, for the constant encouragement and sacrifice on my behalf.

3. Ibid., 238.

"Somebody asked me how I was going to arrange my exhibition," Picasso recalled. "I answered: 'Badly.' Because an exhibition, like a picture, well or badly 'arranged,' means the same thing. That which counts is the spirit of continuity of ideas. And when this spirit exists...everything ends well."[4]

4. Quoted in Basel 1986, N.P.

Judi Freeman

Bibliography

The bibliography of sources on Picasso is vast. The following list is confined to themes particularly relevant to this volume and is annotated accordingly. For a comprehensive compilation of items published through 1975, see Ray Anne Kibbey, *Picasso: A Comprehensive Bibliography* (New York: Garland Press, 1977). Abbreviated citations are used in endnotes to each chapter.

Alley 1986
Alley, Ronald. *Picasso: "The Three Dancers."* London: The Tate Gallery, 1986.
A concise study of the 1925 painting.

Anguera 1979
Anguera, A. Oriol. *Guernica.* Paris: Société française du livre, 1979. Includes rare photographs of Picasso and Dora Maar.

Archambault 1944
Archambault, G. H. "Picasso." *The New York Times Magazine*, (29 October 1944): 18–19, 39. Discusses Picasso's wartime activities and his work following the liberation of Paris.

Arles 1991
Arles, Espace Van Gogh. *Picasso: La Provence & Jacqueline.* Exh. cat, 1991. Organized by Pierre Daix; includes a useful section on Picasso's 1937 images of Lee Miller.

Arnheim 1962
Arnheim, Rudolf. *The Genesis of a Painting: Picasso's "Guernica."* Berkeley: University of California Press, 1962. A formal analysis accompanied by philosophical ruminations on creativity.

Baden-Baden 1969
Baden-Baden, Staatliche Kunsthalle. *Maler und Modell.* Exh. cat, 1969.

Barr 1939
Barr, Alfred H., Jr. *Picasso: Forty Years of His Art.* New York: The Museum of Modern Art, 1939.

Barr 1946
———. *Picasso: Fifty Years of His Art.* New York: The Museum of Modern Art, 1946. The classic study on Picasso's life and work, based on extensive interviews with the artist.

Basel 1986
Basel, Galerie Beyeler. *Picasso: Der Maler und seine Modelle.* Exh. cat., 1986. In German and French, with commentary by Pierre Daix. The focus is on images of women.

Baudin 1977
Baudin, Jacques. "Picasso: Les femmes du diable." *Elle* 1662 (14 November 1977): 50–51. On the role of Marie-Thérèse Walter in Picasso's life and art.

Bellomy 1992
Bellomy, Irene Guenther. "Art and Politics during the German Occupation of France, 1940–1944." Master's thesis, University of Houston, 1992. A useful compendium of secondary research on the art world in France during the German occupation.

Berger 1965
Berger, John. *The Success and Failure of Picasso.* New York: Pantheon Books, 1965. A rich critical assessment examining Picasso's isolation and loneliness and the effect on his oeuvre.

Berlin 1975
Berlin, Neue Gesellschaft für Bildende Kunst. *"Guernica": Kunst und Politik am Beispiel Guernica.* Exh. cat., 1975. Concerned with the responses to Picasso's *Guernica* and the actual events in the town.

Berlin 1992
Berlin, Nationalgalerie. *Picasso: Die Zeit nach "Guernica" 1937–1973.* Exh. cat., 1992. Begins with the images surrounding *Guernica*, including a special section on the weeping women, and continues until the artist's death. The essay by Werner Spies, based on clippings he found in Picasso's archives at the Musée Picasso, is particularly good.

Bernadac 1991
Bernadac, Marie-Laure. *Picasso visages.* Exh. cat. Paris: Musée Picasso, 1991. Photographs of Picasso, accompanied by interviews with the photographers.

Bielefeld 1988
Bielefeld, Kunsthalle. *Picassos Klassizismus: Werke von 1914–1934.* Exh. cat., 1988. Surveys Picasso's classically inspired work in all media.

Bielefeld 1991
———. *Picassos Surrealismus: Werke 1925–1937.* Exh. cat., 1991. A thorough study that includes essays on Picasso and Bataille by Dorothy Kosinski and an analysis of Picasso's writings by Lydia Gasman.

Blake 1983.
Blake, Jody. "The Paintings within Picasso's Paintings." *Athanor* 3 (1983): 67–71. An in-depth study of Picasso's *Bust of a Woman with Self-Portrait* (1929) and *Figure and Profile* (1927–8).

Blunt 1969
Blunt, Anthony. *Picasso's "Guernica."* New York: Oxford University Press, 1969.

Boeck and Sabartés 1955
Boeck, Wilhelm and Jaime Sabartés. *Picasso.* New York: Harry N. Abrams, 1955. A general biography; Sabartés was Picasso's principal confidant.

Bois 1988
Bois, Yves-Alain. "Painting as Trauma." *Art in America* 76, no. 6 (June 1988): 131–73. Reviews the Musée Picasso exhibition devoted to *Les Demoiselles d'Avignon* and proposes a psychoanalytic reading of the painting.

Bornstein 1984
Bornstein, Marc H. "Developmental Psychology and the Problem of Artistic Change." *Journal of Aesthetics and Art Criticism* 43, no. 1 (Winter 1984): 131–45. Considers Picasso's stylistic changes in relation to issues in developmental psychology.

Bozo 1980
Bozo, Dominique. "Le Modèle en question: sur quelques portraits 1930–1940." *Le Courrier de l'Unesco* (December 1980): 47–50. The conflict between tenderness and terror in Picasso's 1930s portraits of women.

Brassaï 1935
Brassaï. "Conversation avec Picasso." *Cahiers d'art* 10 (1935): 173–8. Accompanied by photographs Brassaï had taken since 1932.

Brassaï 1964
———. *Conversations avec Picasso.* Paris: Gallimard, 1964. Brassaï began photographing and talking with Picasso in 1932; this volume is a collection of his writings on the artist.

Breton 1935
Breton, André. "Picasso poète." *Cahiers d'art* 10 (1935): 185–91. Evaluates Picasso's poetry.

Brunner 1988
Brunner, Kathleen. "Picasso in England, 1936–46." Master's thesis, Courtauld Institute of Art, University of London, 1988. Appendix II is an assessment of the English translations of Picasso's poetry.

Brussels 1956
Brussels, Palais des Beaux-Arts. *Picasso: "Guernica."* [in French] Exh. cat., 1956.

Burgard 1986
Burgard, Timothy Anglin. "Picasso's *Night Fishing at Antibes*: Autobiography, Apocalypse, and the Spanish Civil War." *Art Bulletin* 68, no. 4 (December 1986): 657–72.

Cabanne 1974
Cabanne, Pierre. "Picasso et les joies de la paternité." *L'Oeil* 226 (May 1974): 2–11. Interview with Marie-Thérèse Walter just prior to her suicide.

Cabanne 1975
———. *Le siècle de Picasso.* 4 vols. Paris: Editions Denöel, 1975. A sweeping though sporadically documented biography, organized according to stylistic phases of Picasso's career.

Carmean 1980
Carmean, E.A., Jr. *Picasso: "The Saltimbanques."* Exh. cat. Washington, D.C.: National Gallery of Art, 1980. An analysis of the 1905 painting and related works.

Caws et al. 1991
Caws, Mary Ann, Rudolf Kuenzli, and Gwen Raaberg, eds. *Surrealism and Women.* Cambridge, Massachusetts: The MIT Press, 1991. On the work of surrealist women artists and the image of women in surrealist art.

Chadwick 1985
Chadwick, Whitney. *Women Artists and the Surrealist Movement.* Boston: Little, Brown, 1985. The definitive source on women surrealist artists; includes useful section on Dora Maar.

Chipp 1973
Chipp, Herschel B. "*Guernica*: Love, War, and the Bullfight." *Art Journal* 33 (Winter 1973/74): 100–15. Early version of ideas contained in Chipp's later book on the painting.

Chipp 1980
———. "*Guernica*: Once a Document of Outrage, Now a Symbol of Reconciliation in a New and Democratic Spain." *ArtNews* 79, no. 5, (May 1980): 108–12. Parallels the arrival of *Guernica* in the United States in 1939 with its anticipated return to Spain in 1981.

Chipp 1988A
———. *Picasso's "Guernica": History, Transformation, Meanings.* Berkeley: University of California Press, 1988. A comprehensive study of the events in Guernica, the making of the painting, and its impact once completed.

Chipp 1988B
———. "The First Step toward *Guernica*." *Arts Magazine* 63, no. 2, (October 1988): 62–67. Excerpt from Chipp's book, linking the painting to Picasso's images of the artist and his model.

Cleveland 1992
Cleveland, Museum of Art. *Picasso & Things.* Exh. cat., 1992. Exhibition of Picasso's still lifes, with superb catalogue entries and an incisive essay by Marie-Laure Bernadac on Picasso's references to food in his writings.

Cogniat n.d.
Cogniat, Raymond. *Picasso: Figures.* [in French] Lausanne: International Art Books, n.d. Collection of little-known figure paintings by Picasso.

Cohen 1988
Cohen, Ronny H. "Mass Media: Pablo's American Image." *Art in America* 68, no. 10 (December 1980): 43–47. An interesting account of perceptions of Picasso before, during, and after World War II.

Cologne 1988
Cologne, Museum Ludwig. *Picasso im zweiten Weltkrieg 1939 bis 1945.* Exh. cat., 1988. Picasso's activities and work during World War II.

Cone 1992
Cone, Michèle C. *Artists under Vichy: A Case of Prejudice and Persecution.* Princeton: Princeton University Press, 1992. A highly controversial discussion of artists working in occupied France. Includes a section on Picasso—considered by Cone to be a "have," with little deprivation during the war—in relation to the "have not" artists struggling to survive, such as Jean Arp, Sonia Delaunay, Victor Brauner, and Hans Bellmer.

Cooper 1976
Cooper, Douglas. *Pour Eugenia: une suite de 24 dessins inédits exécutés en 1918.* Paris: Berggruen, 1976.

Cowling 1985
Cowling, Elizabeth. "'Proudly We Claim Him as One of Us': Breton, Picasso, and the Surrealist Movement." *Art History* 8, no. 1 (March 1985): 82–104. Examines André Breton's attempts to lure Picasso into the surrealist group during the period from 1922 to 1930.

Crespelle 1969
Crespelle, Jean-Paul. *Picasso and His Women.* Trans. by Robert Baldick. New York: Coward-McCann, 1969.

Crespelle 1971
———. "Les sept femmes de la vie de Picasso." *Elle*, 1349–51 (25 October): 88–93; (1 November): 100–109; (8 November): 100–105. With sections on Marie-Thérèse Walter and Dora Maar.

Crespelle and Saurat 1981
Crespelle, Jean-Paul and Marie-France Saurat. "Le siècle de Picasso." *Paris-Match*, (20 November 1981) n.p. On the seven principal women associated with Picasso: Fernande Olivier, Eva Gouel (Marcelle Humbert), Olga Koklova, Marie-Thérèse Walter, Dora Maar, Françoise Gilot, and Jacqueline Roque.

Daix 1983
Daix, Pierre. "On a Hidden Portrait of Marie-Thérèse." *Artforum*, 22, no. 1 (September 1983): 124–29. Uncovers the hidden references to Marie-Thérèse Walter in a still life from 1925–26.

Daix 1988
———. "Dread, Desire, and the Demoiselles." *ArtNews*, 87, no. 6 (Summer 1988): 133–37. Assesses the development of Picasso's *Les Demoiselles d'Avignon* in light of the then newly-unearthed sketchbooks for the painting.

Daix 1993
———. *Picasso: Life and Art.* Trans. by Olivia Emmet. New York: HarperCollins, 1993. Originally published as *Picasso créateur: La vie intime et l'oeuvre* (Paris: Editions du Seuil, 1987). A comprehensive biography by one of the foremost French Picasso scholars.

Darr 1966
Darr, William. "Images of Eros and Thanatos in Picasso's *Guernica.*" *Art Journal* 25 (Summer 1966): 338–46. Interprets the painting in light of Sigmund Freud's *Civilization and Its Discontents* (1929).

Dijkstra
Dijkstra, Bram. "Painting and Ideology: Picasso and *Guernica.*" *Praxis* 3 (1976): 141–53. Assesses the painting as a twentieth century political and moral symbol.

Dorléac 1993
Dorléac, Laurence Bertrand. *L'art de la défaite 1940–44.* Paris: Editions du Seuil, 1993. A comprehensive study of art under the occupation, by France's foremost art historian.

Dracoulidès 1975
Dracoulidès, N.N. "Investigations or the Mystery of Picasso." *Psychiatry and Art* 4 (1975): 280. Posits that Picasso was a blue baby, because his umbilical cord was wrapped around his neck at birth.

Dracoulidès 1981
———. "Les trois femmes de Picasso." *Arts* 37–38 (16 October 1981): 5; (23 October 1981): 18. Examines the three women in Picasso's life in 1935: Olga Koklova, Marie-Thérèse Walter, and Dora Maar.

Duncan 1961
Duncan, David Douglas. *Picasso's Picassos.* New York: Harper & Brothers, 1961. Photographs taken by Duncan of the artist's home and studio at La Californie. These photographs document some of the thousands of works that would eventually be part of the gift made by Picasso's heirs to France.

Ehrenwald 1963
Ehrenwald, Jan, M.D. "Picasso, Father and Son: Patterns of Contagion and Rebellion in Genius." In *Neurosis in the Family and Patterns of Psychosocial Defense: A Study of Psychiatric Epidemiology*, 109–24. New York: Hoeber Medical Divisions, Harper & Row, 1963. Links events from Picasso's early childhood —in particular, his relationship with his father— to his motifs.

Elsen 1969
Elsen, Albert. "The Many Faces of Picasso's Sculpture." *Art International* 13, no. 6 (Summer 1969): 24–34, 76. A survey of Picasso's sculptural portraits.

Eluard 1935
Eluard, Paul. "Je parle de ce qui est bien." *Cahiers d'art* 10 (1935): 165–8. Eluard discusses Picasso's recent work.

Eluard 1938
———. "La victoire de Guernica," trans. by Roland Penrose, *London Bulletin*, 1, no. 6 (October 1938): 7–8.

Eluard 1947
———. *Pablo Picasso.* trans. by Joseph T. Shipley. New York: Philosophical Library, 1947. Eluard's poetic texts illustrated by the works that inspired them.

Failing 1977
Failing, Patricia. "Picasso's 'Cries of Children...Cries of Stones.'" *ArtNews* 75, no. 7 (September 1977): 55–64. The most thorough analysis of *Dream and Lie of Franco.*

Fernandez Cuenca 1971
Fernandez Cuenca, Carlos. *Picasso en el ciné tambien.* Madrid: Editora Nacional, 1971.

Ferrier 1985
Ferrier, Jean-Louis. *De Picasso à Guernica: Généalogie d'un tableau.* Paris: Denoël, 1985. Reconstructs the events leading up to the painting of *Guernica* and publishes much of the newspaper coverage of its public presentation.

FitzGerald 1992
FitzGerald, Michael C. "Picasso: In the Beaux Quartiers." *Art in America* 80, no. 12 (December 1992): 82–93; 61–63. An article on the 1992 exhibition *Picasso & Things.*

Frascina 1986
Frascina, Francis. "*Guernica*, an Emblem for Spaniards: Picasso, Spain, and Modernism." *Studio International* 199, no. 1012 (1986): 38–42. Describes the significance of Picasso's *Guernica* for Spaniards, from the 1930s until its return to Spain in 1981.

Freedberg 1986
Freedberg, Catherine B. *The Spanish Pavilion at the Paris World's Fair of 1937.* New York: Garland, 1986. Chronicles the conception and construction of the Spanish pavilion.

Gagnebin 1992
Gagnebin, Murielle. "Erotique de Picasso." *Esprit* 61, no. 1 (1992): 71–76.
On Picasso's etchings for Honoré de Balzac's *Le Chef-d'oeuvre inconnu* (1931).

Galassi 1982
Galassi, Susan Grace. "Picasso's *The Lovers* of 1919." *Arts Magazine* 56, no. 2 (February 1982): 76–82.
Analyzes the personal dimensions of the painting.

Gardner 1993
Gardner, Paul. "Picasso: 'You Can Never Write "The End."'" *ArtNews* 92, no.4 (April 1993).

Gasman 1981
Gasman, Lydia. "Mystery, Magic, and Love in Picasso, 1925–1938: Picasso and the Surrealist Poets." Ph.D. diss., Columbia University, 1981.
The single most important work on mid-career Picasso. Gasman interviewed Marie-Thérèse Walter before her death and her conclusions are based on a thorough knowledge of surrealist poetry, literature, and Picasso's writings.

Gedo 1972
Gedo, Mary Mathews. "Picasso's Self-image: A Psycho-Iconographic Study of the Artist's Life and Works." Ph.D. diss., Northwestern University, 1972.
A highly speculative account of Picasso's personality in relation to his work.

Gedo 1979
———. "Art as Autobiography: Picasso's *Guernica*." *Art Quarterly* 2, no. 2 (Spring 1979): 191–210.
Interprets *Guernica* as a political allegory and an expression of the powerful emotions preoccupying the artist.

Gedo 1980 A
———. *Picasso: Art as Autobiography*. Chicago: The University of Chicago Press, 1980.
A psychoanalytic biography.

Gedo 1980B
———. "Art as Exorcism: Picasso's *Demoiselles d'Avignon*." *Arts Magazine,* 55, no. 2 (October 1980): 70–83.
Attempts to explain the outbreak of ferocity that characterizes the painting.

Gettings 1985
Gettings, Frank. "Forum: Picasso's *Portrait of Dora Maar*." *Drawing* 7, no. 1 (May-June 1985): 10.
An analysis of Picasso's 1938 drawing, now in the collection of the Hirshhorn Museum.

Gilot 1990
Gilot, Françoise. *Matisse and Picasso: A Friendship in Art*. New York: Doubleday, 1990. A personal account, written by Picasso's mistress from 1946 to 1954.

Gilot and Lake 1964
Gilot, Françoise and Carlton Lake. *Life with Picasso*. New York: Anchor Books/ Doubleday, 1964.
A firsthand account.

Glimcher and Glimcher 1986
Glimcher, Arnold and Marc Glimcher, eds. *Je Suis le Cahier: The Sketchbooks of Picasso*. Boston and New York: The Atlantic Monthly Press, 1986.
Documents six key sketchbooks of Picasso's in volume accompanying a traveling exhibition.

Glózer 1974
Glózer, László. *Picasso und der Surrealismus*. Cologne: Verlag M. DuMont Schauberg, 1974.

Goggin 1985
Goggin, Mary-Margaret. "Picasso and His Art during the German Occupation: 1940-1944." Ph.D. diss., Stanford University, 1985.
Places Picasso's wartime work in relation to the Occupation of Paris.

Golding 1985
Golding, John. "Picasso & Poetry." *The New York Review of Books* 32, no. 18 (21 November 1985): 11-15.
Examines Picasso's 1948 poem *Góngora*.

Gonçalves 1974
Gonçalves, Rui Mário. "Guernica e os mitos." *Colóquio* 16, no. 16 (February 1974): 18-25.
Analysis of *Guernica* in relation to Picasso's earlier work of the 1930s.

Gopnik 1981-82
Gopnik, Adam. "P Loves MT: A Note on the First Appearance of Marie-Thérèse Walter in the Picasso Theater." *Marsyas* 21 (1981-82): 57-60.
On the cryptic references in Picasso's 1927-28 paintings and drawings.

Gottlieb 1981
Gottlieb, Carla. "Picasso as a Self-Portraitist." *Colóquio* 50 (September 1981): 14-23.
Classifies Picasso's self-portraits into "recognizable and unrecognizable images," "embraced self-portraits," "borrowed bodies," and "metaphorical images."

Grass 1991
Grass, Günter. "*Guernica* Dishonoured." *The Art Newspaper* 8 (May 1991): 10.
Critiques the German government's use of *Guernica* as a recruitment tool for the German armed forces.

Haesserts 1939
Haesserts, Paul. *Picasso et le goût de paroxysme*. Anberes-Amsterdam: Het Kompas, 1939.

Haus 1975-76
Haus, Andreas. "Das Ich und der Andere: 'Existenzielle' Thematik im Werk Pablo Picassos." *Sitzungsberichte: Kunstgeschichtliche Gesellschaft zu Berlin* 24 (October 1975-June 1976): 15-20.
Examines existential themes in Picasso's oeuvre.

Held 1988
Held, Jutta. "How Do the Political Effects of Pictures Come About? The Case of Picasso's *Guernica*." *Oxford Art Journal* 11, no.1 (1988): 33-39.
Discusses the effect of *Guernica* on the Popular Fronts in Spain and France and on American avant-garde circles in the late 1930s and 1940s.

Heydenreich 1979
Heydenreich, Titus. "'Kilómetros y leguas de palabras...': Pablo Picasso als Schriftsteller." *Romantische Zeitschrift für Literaturgeschichte. Cahiers d'histoire des littératures romanes* 3, nos. 1–2 (1979): 154–68.
An evaluation of Picasso's writings.

Hobhouse 1988
Hobhouse, Janet. "Picasso's Nudes." *Connoisseur* 218, no. 921 (October 1988): 172–79.

Hodin 1972
Hodin, J.P. "The Hell of Initiation: An Essay Prompted by a Conversation with C.G. Jung." In *Modern Art and the Modern Man*, 57-96. Cleveland: The Press of Case Western Reserve University, 1972.
Evaluates Jung's commentary on Picasso and James Joyce.

Hohl 1979
Hohl, Reinhold. "Ein Weltbild der Grausamkeit: Picassos *Guernica* und Artauds *Théâtre de la cruauté*." *Frankfurter Allgemeine Zeitung* 280 (1 December 1979): 29.
Compares aspects of Picasso's and Artaud's work.

Hohl 1981
———. "Ich stehe für das Lebel ein gegen den Tod: *Guernica* und die Vorprojekte für den spanischen Pavillon von 1937." *Neue Zürcher Zeitung* 247 (24/25 October 1981): 65-66. Discusses the origins of *Guernica*, its appearance at the International Exposition of 1937, and its eventual home at the Prado.

Hohl 1983
———. "C.G. Jung on Picasso (and Joyce)." *Source: Notes on the History of Art* 3, no. 1 (Fall 1983): 10-18. Recounts the history of Jung's paper occasioned by the 1932 exhibition at the Kunsthaus, Zurich.

Hollier 1989
Hollier, Denis. "Portrait de l'artiste en son absence." *Les Cahiers du Musée national d'art moderne* 30 (Winter 1989): 5-22. Considers Picasso in relation to Georges Bataille. Also looks at his depictions of models.

Houdebine 1981
Houdebine, Jean-Louis. "Jung et Picasso: le déni de l'exception." *Tel Quel* 90 (Winter 1981): 45-55. Discusses Jung's commentary on Picasso; additional conjectures about views of Jung and Freud.

Hubert 1984
Hubert, Renée Riese. "Surrealist Women Painters, Feminist Portraits." *Dada and Surrealism* 13 (1984): 70-82.

Huffington 1988
Huffington, Arianna Stassinopoulos. *Picasso: Creator and Destroyer.* New York: Simon and Schuster, 1988. Widely criticized biography, especially dependent on interviews with Françoise Gilot.

Hugnet 1935
Hugnet, Georges. "L'Iconoclaste." *Cahiers d'art* 10 (1935): 218-20. On Picasso's surrealism.

Jahan 1973
Jahan, Pierre. "Ma première rencontre avec Picasso." *Gazette des beaux-arts* 150 année, 6 sér, vol. 82 (October 1973): 233-36. Recounts a meeting with Picasso in 1944.

Jakovsky 1946
Jakovsky, Anatole. "Midis avec Picasso." *Arts de France* 6 (1946): 3-14. An interview.

Janis and Janis 1946
Janis, Harriet and Sidney Janis. *Picasso: The Recent Years, 1939-46.* Garden City, New York: Doubleday & Company, 1946. Published on the occasion of Picasso's first postwar American exhibition.

Jung 1966
Jung, Carl Gustav. "Picasso." In *The Spirit in Man, Art, and Literature,* 135-41. trans. by R. F. C. Hull. Bollingen Series XX. Princeton: Princeton University Press, 1966. Translated version of an article first published in German in *Neue Zürcher Zeitung* in 1932, in response to Picasso's 1932 exhibition at the Kunsthaus, Zurich.

Kahnweiler 1952
Kahnweiler, Daniel-Henry. "Huit entretiens avec Picasso." *Le Point* (October 1952): 22-27. Interviews dating from 2 October 1933 through 16 February 1935.

Kahnweiler 1956
———. "Entretiens avec Picasso." *Quadrum* 2 (2 November 1956): 73-76. Interviews dating from 30 November 1933 through 8 July 1948.

Kahnweiler 1988
———. *Huit entretiens avec Picasso.* Caen, France: L'Echoppe, 1988. A compendium of all of Kahnweiler's interviews.

Karmel 1980
Karmel, Pepe. "Photography: Portraits of the Artist as Picasso." *Art in America* 68, no. 10 (December 1980): 26-29. Review of an exhibition at the International Center of Photography, New York; analyzes photographs made of Picasso throughout his career.

Kennedy 1960
Kennedy, Robert Woods. "Picasso: A Twentieth Century Masque." *The New Republic* 143 (18 July 1960): 10-14. Considers Picasso's portrayal of relations between the sexes.

Kieser 1981A
Kieser, Emil. "Picasso als Erbe Alter Meister—und die Photographie: Interpretationen der Zeichnungsserie *Amor und das Mädchen.*" *Pantheon* 39, no. 3 (July-September 1981): 237-46. Compares Rembrandt's images of the artist and the model to Picasso's; draws other parallels with northern old masters.

Kieser 1981B
———. "Picassos Weise von Liebe und Tod." *Pantheon* 39, no. 4 (October-December 1981): 327-39. Looks at Picasso's minotaurs, rape scenes, and epic themes from the late 1930s onward and relates them to art historical sources.

Kleinfelder 1993
Kleinfelder, Karen L. *The Artist, His Model, Her Image, His Gaze: Picasso's Pursuit of the Model.* Chicago: The University of Chicago Press, 1993. Focuses on the artist-model theme in the graphic works from 1954 through 1970.

Klüver and Martin 1989
Klüver, Billy and Julie Martin. *Kiki's Paris: Artists and Lovers 1900-1930.* New York: Abrams, 1989.

Krahl and Quandt 1974
Krahl, Ilse and Siegfried Quandt. *Guernica, Guernica: Überlegungen, Vorschläge, Materialien zum fächerübergreifenden Unterricht.* Ratingen: A. Henn Verlag, 1974.

Krauss 1980
Krauss, Rosalind. "Re-Presenting Picasso." *Art in America* 68, no. 10 (December 1980): 90-96. Posits collage as a conceptual way for Picasso to reconsider representation throughout his career, not only during the cubist years.

Krauss 1981
———. "In the Name of Picasso." *October* 16 (Spring 1981): 5-21. Inspired by the recent trend in Picasso studies to rely heavily on biographical material to evaluate his work, Krauss posits an alternative reading emphasizing the conceptual and formal features.

Kuspit 1988
Kuspit, Donald. "Surrealism's Re-Vision of Psychoanalysis." In *Psychoanalytic Perspectives on Art*, III, edited by Mary Mathews Gedo, 197-209. London: The Analytic Press, 1988. Considers Breton's notions of psychoanalysis.

Langston 1977
Langston, Linda. "Disguised Double Portraits in Picasso's Work, 1925-1962." Ph.D. diss., Stanford University, 1977. The double portrait and the embrace in Picasso's work, with a special emphasis on depictions of Walter, Koklova, and Maar.

Laporte 1963
Laporte, Paul. "Four Paintings by Picasso." *Los Angeles County Museum of Art Bulletin* 15, no. 3 (1963): 3-13.
On key works by Picasso in the museum's collection. Useful information about the *Weeping Woman with Handkerchief* of 26 June 1937.

Larrea 1947
Larrea, Juan. *"Guernica": Pablo Picasso.* New York: Curt Valentin, 1947.
An incisive account of *Guernica* written shortly after World War II, reprinting Paul Eluard's poem.

Lavin 1993
Lavin, Irving. "Picasso's Bull(s): Art History in Reverse." *Art in America* 81, no. 3 (March 1993): 76-93.
On Picasso's bull imagery in a series of postwar lithographs.

Leighten 1989
Leighten, Patricia. *Re-Ordering the Universe: Picasso and Anarchism 1897-1914.* Princeton: Princeton University Press, 1989.
On Picasso's interest in politics during his blue, rose, and cubist periods.

Leja 1985
Leja, Michael. *"Le vieux marcheur* and *Les deux risques*: Picasso, Prostitution, Venereal Disease, and Maternity, 1899-1907." *Art History* 8, no. 1 (March 1985): 66-81.
A thematic examination of Picasso's earliest works.

Leymarie 1971
Leymarie, Jean. *Picasso: The Artist of the Century.* New York: The Viking Press, 1971.
Includes a very useful section on Picasso's depictions of women.

Lichtenstern 1980
Lichtenstern, Christa. *Picassos "Tête de femme": Zwischen Klassik und Surrealismus.* Exh. cat. Frankfurt am Main: Städelsches Kunstinstitut und Städtische Galerie, 1980.
Comprehensive study of Picasso's *Tête de femme* (1932).

Lipton 1976
Lipton, Eunice. *Picasso Criticism 1901-1939.* New York: Garland, 1976.
Evaluates the literature on Picasso with respect to its ideological roots and associations.

London 1988
London, Tate Gallery. *Late Picasso: Paintings, Sculpture, Drawings, Prints 1953-1972.* Exh. cat., 1988.
A reassessment of Picasso's late work, including a thoughtful essay by John Richardson on Jacqueline Roque.

Lopéz-Rey 1981
Lopéz-Rey, José. "Le *Guernica* de Picasso." *L'Oeil* 315 (October 1981): 36-41.
Traces the origin of several elements in *Guernica* to earlier works.

Lord 1993
Lord, James. *Picasso and Dora: A Memoir.* New York: Farrar, Straus & Giroux, 1993.
Lord, the biographer of Alberto Giacometti, was close to Dora Maar after World War II. This account describes that period in his life.

Lourenço 1974
Lourenço, Eduardo. "O Pintor e a máscara." *Colóquio* 16, no. 16 (February 1974): 14-17.
A brief assessment of Picasso's self-portraits.

MacGregor-Haste 1988
MacGregor-Haste, Roy. *Picasso's Women.* Luton, England: Lennard Publishing, 1988.
A rather sensationalistic account.

Madrid 1987
Madrid, Centro de Arte Reina Sofia. *Pabellón español: Exposición internacional de Paris 1937.* Exh. cat., 1987.
Includes very useful material on the contributions of Picasso, Miró, and González to the Spanish pavilion.

Madrid 1991
Madrid, Fundación Juan March. *Picasso: Retratos de Jacqueline.* Exh. cat., 1991.
An analysis of Picasso's depictions of Jacqueline Roque.

Málaga 1993
Málaga, Palacío Episcopal. *Picasso clásico.* Exh. cat., 1993.
Exhibition, organized by Gary Tinterow and Carmen Giménez, on the classical years in Picasso's career.

Marin 1986
Marin, Juan. *Sous le nom de Guernica: discourse et regards.* Paris: DEA, 1986.

McFadden and Deitch 1980
McFadden, Sarah and Jeffrey Deitch. "The Midas Brush." *Art in America* 68, no. 10 (December 1980): 147-47, 183-85.
Charts the economic aspects of Picasso's career, during and after his lifetime.

Melbourne 1984
Melbourne, National Gallery of Victoria. *Picasso.* Exh. cat., 1984.
Exhibition of works principally from the Marina Picasso collection. Useful essay on Picasso and women: "Painting As If to Possess," by Memory Holloway.

Melville 1940
Melville, Robert. "Picasso's Anatomy of Woman." In *The New Apocalypse: An Anthology of Criticism, Poems and Stories*, edited by Dorian Cooke, et al., 92-100. London: The Fortune Press, 1940.
Discusses drawings from 1927-38 that communicate the erotic and expressive content of Picasso's depictions of women.

Melville 1942
———. "The Evolution of the Double Head in the Art of Picasso." *Horizon* 6, no. 35 (November 1942): 343-51.
Considers the motif from 1925 through 1937.

Mena Marques 1987
Mena Marques, Manuela. "Un precedente italiano en el *Guernica* de Picasso." *Archivo Español de Arte* 118, no. 18 (1987): 165-72. Identifies Vitale da Bologna's *St. George and the Dragon* as a source for the rearing horse in *Guernica*.

Miami 1985
Miami, Center for the Fine Arts. *Picasso at Work at Home: Selections from the Marina Picasso Collection.* Exh. cat., 1985.

Micha 1981
Micha, René. "Le nu comme le nu." *L'Arc* 82 (1981): 1-5.
A concise history of Picasso's nudes.

Mili 1970
Mili, Gjon. *Picasso et la troisième dimension.* Paris: Ed. Triton, 1970.
On Picasso and film.

Munich 1981
Munich, Haus der Kunst. *Pablo Picasso: Eine Ausstellung zum hundertsten Geburtstag.* Exh. cat., 1981.
One hundred works from the Marina Picasso collection, spanning all periods.

New York 1980
New York, The Museum of Modern Art. *Pablo Picasso: A Retrospective.* Exh. cat., 1980.
The catalogue of the mammoth Picasso retrospective of 1980. Contains a generously illustrated chronology by Jane Fluegel.

New York 1985
New York, William Beadleston, Inc., *Through the Eye of Picasso 1928-1934.* Exh. cat., 1985.

New York 1993
New York, Solomon R. Guggenheim Museum. *Picasso and the Age of Iron.* Exh. cat., 1993.
An exhibition tracing the use of iron by Picasso, González, Alexander Calder, and David Smith.

Nieto Alcaide 1990
Nieto Alcaide, Víctor. "El toro del *Guernica*: el relato y la imagen del pintor." *Kalías: revista d'arte 2*, no. 3/4 (October 1990): 66-71.
Associates the bull in *Guernica* with the artist.

Nochlin 1980
Nochlin, Linda. "Picasso's Color: Schemes and Gambits." *Art in America 68*, no. 10 (December 1980): 105-123,177-83.
An essential and, oddly enough, unique article devoted to the very important topic of Picasso's use of color.

Olano 1987
Olano, Antonio B. *Las mujeres de Picasso.* Barcelona: Editorial Planeta, 1987.
Traces (pp. 110-31) Picasso's relationships with Olga Koklova, Marie-Thérèse Walter, and Dora Maar.

Olivier 1988
Olivier, Fernande. *Souvenirs intimes.* Paris: Calman-Lévy, 1988. First published in 1933 as *Picasso et ses amis.* Firsthand account of Picasso's life during the first decade of the twentieth century, by his mistress of the time.

Oppler 1988
Oppler, Ellen C., ed. *Picasso's "Guernica."* New York: W.W. Norton, 1988.
A compendium of primary sources and documents as well as critical studies.

Paris 1955
Paris, Musée des Arts Décoratifs, *Picasso*, exh. cat., 1955.
Catalogue of major Paris retrospective.

Paris 1966-67
Paris, Grand Palais. *Homage à Pablo Picasso.* Exh. cat., 1966-67.
Catalogue of Jean Leymarie's retrospective of the artist, the last major exhibition prior to his death.

Paris 1980
———. *La Vie mystérieuse des chefs-d'oeuvre: la science au service de l'art.* Exh. cat., 1980.
On the results of x-ray studies of Picasso's *Portrait de Marie-Thérèse* (6 January 1937).

Paris 1985
Paris, Musée Picasso. *Catalogue sommaire des collections.* 2 vols. Paris: Ministère de la culture, Editions de la réunion des musées nationaux, 1985.
Two-volume master guide to the Musée Picasso's holdings of paintings, sculptures, collages, reliefs, ceramics, drawings, watercolors, gouaches, and pastels.

Paris 1987
———. *Picasso vu par Brassaï.* Exh. cat., 1987.
Photographs taken by the Hungarian photographer Brassaï of Picasso in his studio during the 1930s and 1940s.

Paris 1988
Paris, Musée de l'Orangerie. *Les Grandes Baigneuses de Picasso.* Exh. cat., 1988.
Considers the paintings in the context of other large female nudes by nineteenth- and twentieth-century artists.

Parmelin 1966
Parmelin, Hélène. *Picasso says....* trans. by Christine Trollope. South Brunswick, New York: A.S. Barnes and Co., 1966.
Picasso on a variety of topics, interspersed with Parmelin's narration. Most of Picasso's statements may be dated between 1962 and 1966, when Parmelin was in frequent contact with him.

Penrose 1967
Penrose, Roland. *The Sculpture of Picasso.* Exh. cat., New York: The Museum of Modern Art, 1967.

Penrose 1971
———. *Portrait of Picasso.* New York: The Museum of Modern Art, 1971.
A concise biography, amply illustrated with documentary photographs.

Penrose 1981A
———. *Picasso: His Life and Work.* 3rd ed. London: Granada, 1981. First published in 1958.
The definitive biography of Picasso by the artist and critic who knew him from the 1930s until his death in 1973.

Penrose 1981B
———. *Scrap Book.* London: Thames and Hudson, 1981.

Penrose and Bozo 1980
Penrose, Roland and Dominique Bozo. "Picasso, the Surrealist Realist: Excerpts from a Conversation between Roland Penrose and Dominique Bozo." *Artforum 19* (September 1980): 24-30.
Discusses Picasso's career generally.

Penrose and Golding 1973
Penrose, Roland and John Golding, eds. *Picasso in Retrospect.* New York: Harper & Row, 1973.
Contains key writings on Picasso by a group of international scholars. Includes Golding's "Picasso and Surrealism," Penrose's "Beauty and the Monster," and Michel Leiris' "The Artist and His Model."

Persin 1991
Persin, Patrick-Gilles. "Pablo Picasso *Femmes au Chapeau*, 1937-48." *Cimaise 38*, no. 215 (1991): 123-26.
On a presentation of these depictions of Dora Maar at the 1991 FIAC (Foire internationale d'art contemporain) in Paris.

Pérussaux 1961
Pérussaux, Charles. "Le Visage de la femme chez Picasso." *La Nouvelle Critique*, special number (November 1961): 46-52.
Very general article on Picasso's depictions of women, with a slight emphasis on the works related to *Guernica.*

"Picasso" 1968
"Picasso." *Life* special double issue (27 December 1968).
Lavishly illustrated biographical essay on Picasso.

"Picasso" 1980
"Picasso: A Symposium." *Art in America 68*, no. 10 (December 1980): 19, 185-87.
Occasioned by the Museum of Modern Art's Picasso retrospective; includes John Jacobus, Clement Greenberg, Edward Ruscha, Joseph Kosuth, Peter Schjeldahl, Larry Rivers, Carter Ratcliff, Lawrence Alloway, Richard Serra, Tony Shafrazi, Eric Fischl, Bruce Boice, Elizabeth Murray, Frederick Wight, Donald B. Kuspit, and Don Celender.

Picasso 1936A
Picasso, Pablo. "Declaraciones de Picasso." *Gaceta de arte* 37 (March 1936): 10-13.
On the occasion of a 1936 exhibition in Tenerife these remarks were recorded by Picasso's friend Christian Zervos.

Picasso 1936B
———. "Poemas inéditos de Picasso." *Gaceta de arte* 37 (March 1936): 17-19.
Two poems, dating from 28 November and 24 December 1935.

Picasso 1936C
———. "Six Poems by Pablo Picasso." Trans. by George Reavey. In *Contemporary Poetry and Prose*, 4-5 (August-September 1936): 75-79.
Poems from 28 November through 24 December 1935, and from 25-29 March 1936.

Picasso 1937
———. "Songe et mensonge de Franco." *Cahiers d'art*, No. 1-3 (1937): 37-50.

Picasso 1944
———. *Poemas y declaraciones*. Mexico City: Darro y Genil, 1944.
Includes poems of 28 November and 5, 6, and 24 December 1935; a collection of fragments; the text of *Sueño y mentira de Franco*; and statements from 1923 and 1935.

Picasso 1945
———. [Untitled statement]. *Picasso libre: 212 peintures 1940-1945*. Exh. cat. Paris: Louis Carré, 1945.
Picasso's conception of the artist.

Picasso 1950
———. *Desire Caught by the Tail*. Trans. by Bernard Frechtman. London: Rider and Company, 1950.
Picasso's play, first performed in 1944.

Picasso 1964
———. "The Wisdom of Pablo Picasso: The World's Foremost Living Artist Puts Forth a Credo for Creativity." *Playboy* 11 (January 1964): 96-98, 236-38.
Assorted translated fragments of statements by Picasso, from unidentified sources.

Picasso 1972
———. *Picasso on Art: A Selection of Views*. Edited by Dore Ashton. New York: Da Capo Press, 1972.
Assorted statements, translated into English and arranged by subject.

Picasso 1989
———. *Collected Writings*. Edited by Marie-Laure Bernadac and Christine Piot. New York: Abbeville Press, 1989.
The written work from 1935 through 1959.

Pleynet 1981
Pleynet, Marcelin. "Picasso peintre d'histoire?" *Tel Quel* 90 (Winter 1981): 21-57.
Guernica as a history painting.

Poggi 1992
Poggi, Christine. *In Defiance of Painting: Cubism, Futurism, and the Invention of Collage*. New Haven: Yale University Press, 1992.

Posada Kubissa 1988
Posada Kubissa, Teresa "Picasso y el cine: *El Guernica* y *El Acorazado Potemkin*." *Boletín del Museo del Prado* 9, no. 25/27 (1988): 110-17.
Compares Picasso's *Guernica* to Sergei Eisenstein's *Potemkin* (1926).

Post 1988
Post, Stephen L., M.D. "Surrealism, Psychoanalysis, and Centrality of Metaphor." In *Psychoanalytic Perspectives on Art*, III, ed. by Mary Mathews Gedo, 177-95. London: The Analytic Press, 1988.

Proweller 1971
Proweller, William. "Picasso's *Guernica*: A Study in Visual Metaphor." *Art Journal* 30 (Spring 1971): 240-48.

Puente 1985
Puente, Joaquín de la. *"Guernica": The Making of a Painting*. Madrid: Silex, 1985.
A basic chronology of the genesis of *Guernica*.

Reff 1980
Reff, Theodore. "Picasso's Three Musicians: Maskers, Artists, and Friends." *Art in America* 68, no. 10 (December 1980): 124-42.
On the iconographic origins and classical inspirations of three figures of the 1920s.

Richardson 1970
Richardson, John. "The Significance of Picasso's Self-Portraits." In *Christie's Review of the Year 1969-70*, ed. by John Herbert, 124-26. London: Hutchinson, 1970.
An examination of Picasso's *Portrait de l'artiste* (1901).

Richardson 1980
———. "Your Show of Shows." *New York Review of Books* 27, no. 12 (17 July 1980): 16-24.
Reviews of the 1980 Picasso exhibitions and *Picasso: The Cubist Years* by Pierre Daix.

Richardson 1985A
———. "Picasso and Marie-Thérèse Walter." In *Through the Eye of Picasso 1928-1934*. Exh. cat. New York: William Beadleston, Inc., 1985.
Picasso's relationship with Walter and his depictions of her.

Richardson 1985B
———. "Picasso and L'Amour Fou." *New York Review of Books* 32, no. 20 (19 December 1985): 59-68. Picasso and Walter.

Richardson 1987A
———. "Picasso's Apocalyptic Whorehouse." *New York Review of Books* 34, no. 7 (23 April 1987): 40-47.
The genesis of *Les Demoiselles d'Avignon*, prompted by the Musée Picasso's exhibition on the subject.

Richardson 1987B
———. "Picasso's Secret Love," *House and Garden* 159, no. 10 (October 1987): 174-83, 252-54.
On Picasso's relationship with Gabrielle Lespinasse.

Richardson 1991
———. *A Life of Picasso*. Volume I, 1881-1906. New York: Random House, 1991.
The best and most thoroughly researched biography to date, by a longstanding friend of the artist.

Richardson 1992
———. "Picasso's Alchemy." *House and Garden* 164, no. 3 (March 1992): 142-47, 170.
Review of the 1992 *Picasso and Things* exhibition.

Rose 1972
Rose, Barbara. "Picasso with Women: Pygmalion to his Galateas." *Vogue* 159 (1 April 1972): 131-34, 169.

Rosenblum 1966
Rosenblum, Robert. "Picasso as a Surrealist." *Artforum* V no. 1 (September 1966): 21-25.

Rosenblum 1977
———. "Picasso's *Woman with a Book*." *Arts Magazine* 51, no. 5 (January 1977): 100-105.
Situates Picasso's 1932 painting in the context of his depictions of women in armchairs, etc.

Rosenblum 1985
———. "The Fatal Women of Picasso and De Kooning." *ArtNews* 84, no. 6 (October 1985): 98-103.
Discusses the convergence of the two artists' depictions; specifically considers the theme of the femme fatale in Picasso's work.

Rovamo 1980
Rovamo, Elisa. "Miten Guernica syntyi?" *Taide* 21, no. 4 (1980): 32-37.
Traces the sketches for *Guernica* and the *Minotauromachy*.

Rubin 1972
Rubin, William. *Picasso in the Collection of The Museum of Modern Art.* New York: The Museum of Modern Art, 1972.
A comprehensive catalogue of MOMA's current and anticipated holdings.

Rubin and Armstrong 1992
Rubin, William S. and Matthew Armstrong. *The William S. Paley Collection.* New York: The Museum of Modern Art, 1992.

Russell 1980
Russell, Frank D. *Picasso's "Guernica": The Labyrinth of Narrative and Vision.* Montclair, New Jersey: Allanheld & Schram, 1980.
An analysis of the painting's individual sections and motifs.

Sabartés 1935
Sabartés, Jaime. "Las literatura de Picasso." *Cahiers d'art* 10 (1935): 225-39.
Analyzes Picasso's poems of 28 November, 6 and 24 December 1935. In Spanish, with French translations of the poems.

Sabartés 1946
———. *Picasso: Portraits et souvenirs.* Paris: Louis Carré, 1946.

Sabartés 1949
———. *Picasso: An Intimate Portrait.* London: W. H. Allen, 1949.

Schaffer 1984
Schaffer, Barbro. "Picassos *Guernica* och den svenska kritiken." *Konsthistorisk Tidskrift* 53, no. 2 (1984): 86-89.
The reception of *Guernica* as recounted in Swedish newspapers and journals.

Scheidegger 1972
Scheidegger, Alfred. "Erotik in der bildenden Kunst—Pablo Picasso." In *Der befreite Eros*, edited by Anton Grabner-Haider and Kurt Lüthe, 165-75. Mainz: Matthias-Grünewald-Verlag, 1972.
Identifies specific phases of Picasso's erotic work: 1900-1907, 1930-37, 1945-48, and 1955-1968.

Schiff 1976
Schiff, Gert. *Picasso in Perspective.* Englewood Cliffs, New Jersey: Prentice-Hall, 1976.
An essential compendium, including Robert Rosenblum's seminal "Picasso and the Anatomy of Eroticism," and James Thrall Soby's "Picasso and Surrealism."

Schiff 1983
———. *Picasso: The Last Years, 1963-1973.* Exh. cat. New York: Grey Art Gallery & Study Center, 1983.
An incisive reassessment of Picasso's late career, previously dismissed by many critics.

Schwarz 1988
Schwarz, Herbert T. *Picasso and Marie-Thérèse Walter, 1925-1927.* Sillery, Québec: Editions Isabeau, Inc., 1988.
A dogged study, designed to determine precisely when Picasso met Marie-Thérèse Walter. The author speculates that the meeting occurred in 1925.

Seckel 1983
Seckel, Curt. "Der gespaltene Kopf im Werk Picassos: Versuch einer Deutung." *Die Kunst und das schöne Heim* 93, no. 11 (November 1983): 748-52.
On double heads.

Seckler 1945
Seckler, Jerome. "Picasso Explains." *New Masses*, 13 March 1945.
Interview by Jerome Seckler at the end of the German Occupation of Paris.

Serraller 1981
Serraller, Francisco Calvo. "El *Guernica* como enigma." *Goya* 164-165 (September-December 1981): 114-19.
Examines the genesis of *Guernica* in the tableaux paintings of Caravaggio, Guido Reni, and Géricault.

Smith 1982
Smith, Laura E. "Iconographic Issues in Picasso's *Women in the Garden.*" *Arts Magazine* 56, no. 5 (January 1982): 142-47.
Interprets Picasso's *Woman in the Garden* (1930-31, painted metal) as an homage to Marie-Thérèse Walter, as well as a monument to Apollinaire.

Sollers 1981
Sollers, Philippe. "De la virilité considérée comme un des beaux-arts." *Tel Quel* 90 (Winter 1981): 16-20.
On the sexual aspects of Picasso's imagery.

Southworth 1977
Southworth, Herbert R. *Guernica! Guernica!: A Study of Journalism, Diplomacy, Propaganda, and History.* Berkeley: University of California Press, 1977.

Spies 1982
Spies, Werner. "Picasso: l'histoire dans l'atelier." *Cahiers du Musée national d'art moderne* 9 (1982): 62-77.
On Picasso's major tableau paintings.

Spies 1983
———. *Picasso: Das plastische Werk.* Exh. cat. Berlin: Nationalgalerie, Staatliche Museen Preussischer Kulturbesitz, 1983.
Catalogue raisonné of Picasso's sculptural oeuvre.

Spies 1988
———. *Kontinent Picasso.* Munich: Prestel-Verlag, 1988.
Spies' essays on Picasso, including texts on *Dream and Lie of Franco* and *Guernica.*

Stein 1970
Stein, Gertrude. *Picasso: The Complete Writings.* Boston: Beacon Press, 1970.
Picasso's collector, patron, friend, and model gives her unique view of the work and life of the artist.

Steinberg 1988
Steinberg, Leo. "The Philosophical Brothel." *October* 44 (Spring 1988): 7-74.
Originally published in *ArtNews*, September-October 1972, then subsequently in catalogue for *Les Demoiselles d'Avignon* exhibition (1988). This version contains revisions of both previous texts, with new footnotes and fresh analysis based on new preparatory works that have emerged.

Steinberg 1989
Steinberg, Leo. "La Fin de partie de Picasso." *Les Cahiers du Musée national d'art moderne* 27 (Spring 1989): 11-28.
On the late work of Picasso, with an interesting section devoted to double, bifurcated portraits.

Stich 1977
Stich, Sidra. "Toward a Modern Mythology: Picasso and Surrealism." Ph.D. diss., University of California at Berkeley, 1977.
Situates Picasso's work in the midst of the political, social, and aesthetic turmoil in Paris in the 1920s and 1930s.

Tankard 1984
Tankard, Alice Doumanian. *Picasso's "Guernica" after Rubens's "Horrors of War": A Comparative Study in Three Parts—Iconographic and Compositional, Stylistic, and Psychoanalytic.* Philadelphia: The Art Alliance Press, 1984. Contains highly speculative psychoanalytic chapter, "Picasso on the Art Historian's Couch."

Tinterow 1981
Tinterow, Gary. *Master Drawings by Picasso.* New York: George Braziller, and Cambridge, Massachusetts: Fogg Art Museum, 1981. A very fine selection, accompanied by excellent catalogue entries.

Tokyo 1962
Tokyo, National Museum of Western Art. *Picasso: "Guernica".* Exh. cat., 1962. An exhibition of the mural with all of its sketches.

Tokyo 1981
Tokyo, Seibu Museum of Art. *Picasso in time: Collection Maya Ruiz-Picasso.* Exh. Cat., 1981. Includes rarely seen photographs and documents of Marie-Thérèse Walter.

Tuchman 1983
Tuchman, Phyllis. "Guernica and *Guernica*." *Artforum* 21, no. 3 (April 1983): 44-51. Analyzes the painting in relation to news accounts of what was happening in the village.

Turner 1984
Turner, Elizabeth Hutton. "Who Is In the Brothel of Avignon? A Case for Context." *Artibus et Historiae* 9 (1984): 139-57. Relates the sketches for *Les Demoiselles d'Avignon* to the preparation of the final version of the painting.

Ullman 1985
Ullmann, Ludwig. "Zur Vorgeschichte von Picassos *Guernica*, I: Unbekannte und unbeachtete Arbeiten (Januar-April 1937)." *Kritische Berichte* 13, no. 4 (1985): 45-56. Traces the metamorphosis of Picasso's *Guernica* in little-known sketchbook drawings from 1937.

Ullman 1986A
———. "Zur Vorgeschichte von Picassos *Guernica*, II: Entwürfe zu einem Atelier-Bild." *Kritische Berichte* 14, no. 1 (1986): 4-26. Traces the metamorphosis of Picasso's *Guernica* from an image of the artist in his studio to the final painting.

Ullman 1986B
———. "Der Krieg im Werk Picassos." 2 vols. Ph.D. diss., Universität Osnabrück, 1986. Surveys Picasso's references to war. Devotes several pages (158–162) to the theme of the weeping women.

Valencia 1984
Valencia, Valencia Generalitat. *El "Guernica" de Picasso.* Exh. cat., 1984. Includes useful essay, "*Guernica*: History and Symbol," by Román de la Calle.

Varnedoe 1976
Varnedoe, Kirk. "The Self and Others in Modern Portraits." *ArtNews* 75, no. 8 (October 1976): 64-70. Picasso in the context of twentieth-century portraits.

Verdet 1952
Verdet, André. *Faunes et nymphes de Pablo Picasso.* Geneva: Editions Pierre Cailler, 1952. Poetic observations on the postwar sculptures of fauns and nymphs.

Vergine 1982
Vergine, Lea. *L'Autre moitié de l'avant-garde 1910/1940: femmes peintures et femmes sculpteurs dans les mouvements d'avant garde historique.* Paris: Des femmes, 1982. Good source on women avant-garde artists in France, with a useful section on Dora Maar.

Warnod 1945
Warnod, André. "En peinture tout n'est que signe, nous dit Picasso." *Arts* 22 (29 June 1945): 1,4. Interview.

Wiesel 1986
Wiesel, Miriam J. "Picassolysiert." *Wolkenkratzer Art Journal* 12, no. 2 (April-June 1986): 68–69. A brief assessment of art historian Max Imdahl's writings on Picasso's *Guernica*.

Weiss and Ocaña 1992
Weiss, Evelyn, and Maria Teresa Ocaña, eds. *Picasso: The Ludwig Collection.* Munch: Prestel-Verlag, 1992. Comprehensive guide to the holdings at the Ludwig Museum, Cologne.

Wilson 1989
Wilson, Sarah. "Collaboration in the Fine Arts, 1940–1944." In *Collaboration in France: Politics and Culture during the Nazi Occupation, 1940-1944*, ed. by Gerhard Hirschfeld and Patrick Marsh, 103–25. Oxford: Berg Publishers, 1989.

Yaffe 1987
Yaffe, Phyllis Cohen. "The 'Artist and Model' Theme in Picasso's Work between 1926 and 1963." Ph.D. diss., McGill University, 1987. Especially good on Picasso's work in the 1920s.

Zervos 1932-78
Zervos, Christian. *Pablo Picasso.* 33 vols. Paris: Cahiers d'art, [1932]-1978. Catalogue raisonné of the artist's work.

Zervos 1935
———. "Conversation avec Picasso." *Cahiers d'art* 10 (1935): 173–78. Interview, later issued in English and Spanish. Reprinted in Barr 1946.

Zervos 1945
———. "Picasso: figures d'entre deux charniers." *Art in America* 2 (1945): 52-55. On Picasso's portraits during the war.

County of Los Angeles

Board of Supervisors, 1994

Yvonne Brathwaite Burke
Chairman

Michael D. Antonovich
Deane Dana
Edmund D. Edelman
Gloria Molina

Acting Chief Administrative Officer and Director of Personnel

Sally Reed

Los Angeles County Museum of Art Board of Trustees

Fiscal Year 1993–94

Daniel N. Belin
Chairman

Robert F. Maguire III
President

Julian Ganz, Jr.
Chairman of the Executive Committee

James R. Young
Secretary | Treasurer

Mrs. Howard Ahmanson
William H. Ahmanson
Howard P. Allen
Robert O. Anderson
Mrs. Lionel Bell
Dr. George N. Boone
Donald L. Bren
Mrs. Willard Brown
Mrs. B. Gerald Cantor
Mrs. William M. Carpenter
Mrs. Edward W. Carter
Hans Cohn
Robert A. Day
Michael R. Forman
Mrs. Camilla Chandler Frost
David Geffen
Herbert M. Gelfand
Arthur Gilbert
Stanley Grinstein
Robert H. Halff
Felix Juda

Mrs. Dwight M. Kendall
Cleon T. Knapp
Mrs. Harry Lenart
Eric Lidow
Herbert L. Lucas, Jr.
Steve Martin
William A. Mingst
Sergio Muñoz
Mrs. David Murdock
Dr. Franklin D. Murphy
Mrs. Barbara Pauley Pagen
Mrs. Stewart Resnick
Hiroyuki Saito
Dr. Richard A. Simms
Michael G. Smooke
Ray Stark
Frederick R. Weisman
Walter L. Weisman
David L. Wolper
Julius L. Zelman
Selim K. Zilkha

Honorary Life Trustees
Robert H. Ahmanson
The Honorable Walter H. Annenberg
Mrs. Anna Bing Arnold
R. Stanton Avery
B. Gerald Cantor
Edward W. Carter
Mrs. Freeman Gates
Joseph B. Koepfli
Mrs. Rudolph Liebig
Mrs. Lucille Ellis Simon
Mrs. Lillian Apodaca Weiner

Past Presidents
Edward W. Carter
1961–66

Sidney F. Brody
1966–70

Dr. Franklin D. Murphy
1970–74

Richard E. Sherwood
1974–78

Mrs. F. Daniel Frost
1978–82

Julian Ganz, Jr.
1982–86

Daniel N. Belin
1986–90

RITTER LIBRARY
BALDWIN-WALLACE COLLEGE